W9-BEQ-411

BABIES

> **NOTE**
> This publication was written by a registered dietitian to provide insights into better eating habits to promote health and wellness for your baby. It is not a substitute for the advice and/or treatment given by a licensed physician.

First published in French in 2016 by Les Publications Modus Vivendi Inc. under the title *Bébés*.
© Stéphanie Côté and Les Publications Modus Vivendi Inc., 2016

MODUS VIVENDI PUBLISHING
55 Jean-Talon Street West
Montreal, Quebec H2R 2W8
CANADA

modusvivendipublishing.com

Publisher: Marc G. Alain
Editorial director: Isabelle Jodoin
Content and copy editor: Nolwenn Gouezel
English-language editor: Carol Sherman
Translator: Rhonda Mullins
English-language copy editor: Maeve Haldane
Graphic designer: Émilie Houle
Food photographer: André Noël (anoelphoto.com)
Food stylist: Gabrielle Dalessandro
Author photographer: David Moore (artistikdaimo.com)

Additional photography:

Pages 50, 52, 55, 72, 89 (top right), 100 (top left), 107, 110, 116, 118, 123, 172 and 206: Camille Gyrya (camillegyrya.com)

Pages 5, 6, 9, 10, 13, 15, 21, 22, 24, 25, 26, 28, 30, 32, 35, 37, 39, 41, 45, 47, 53, 56, 57, 58, 63, 65, 67, 69, 70, 75, 77, 81, 82, 83, 84, 85, 86, 87, 89 (middle and bottom), 90, 91, 92, 93, 94, 95, 97, 98, 99, 100 (top right, middle and bottom), 101, 102, 103, 106, 108, 115, 122, 124, 126, 130, 135, 136, 138, 139, 145, 150, 152, 155, 158, 160, 166, 170, 176, 185, 190, 192, 202 and 205: iStock

ISBN: 978-1-77286-042-9 (PAPERBACK)

ISBN: 978-1-77286-043-6 (PDF)
ISBN: 978-1-77286-044-3 (EPUB)
ISBN: 978-1-77286-045-0 (KINDLE)

Legal deposit – Bibliothèque et Archives nationales du Québec, 2016
Legal deposit – Library and Archives Canada, 2016

All rights reserved. No part of this publication may be reproduced, stored in a retrieval system or transmitted, in any form or by any means, without the publisher's written authorization.

We gratefully acknowledge the financial support of the Government of Canada through the Canada Book Fund for our publishing activities.

Government of Quebec – Tax Credit for Book Publishing – Program administered by SODEC

Printed in Canada

KNOW WHAT TO EAT

BABIES

21 DAYS OF MENUS

Stéphanie Côté, MSc, RD

MODUS VIVENDI

CONTENTS

After birth, babies are fed only liquids. Whether breast milk or formula, the approach is relatively simple: you feed them when they are hungry. But as they grow, milk is no longer enough for their needs. They are ready for food. And that's when the questions come up! What food group should you start with? Are there foods to avoid? What form should the new food be served in? How often? How much? How do you make purées? What do you do if they don't like it? And the list goes on.

Knowledge and recommendations about feeding babies keep changing. Between advice found online and advice from your mother, your mother-in-law, your friends and even your hairdresser, it can be hard to figure out what's right. That is the purpose of this book. It explains the dietary needs of babies and how to meet them.

The first part of this guide includes important information about the nutritional needs of babies and introducing complementary foods, from the choice of ingredients to preparing them to help children develop their tastes and eat their fill. The second part has 21 days of sample menus adapted to the baby's age (7 to 8 months, 9 to 11 months and 12 to 18 months). The third part offers over 50 recipes designed for little ones who are discovering food and to teach them the pleasure of eating well.

Eating well is good for your health and your taste buds. It's a pleasure that's learned!

FEEDING BABIES

Feeding babies of course means serving them food that helps them grow in good health, delivering the nutrition they need. But it also means letting them make discoveries with all of their senses (sight, touch, smell, hearing and taste), developing their tastes, listening to their body (knowing when they are hungry and when they are full) and spending time at the table with their family.

Children form a positive opinion of food when they associate it with a good experience. Food they discover in a pleasant atmosphere is more likely to end up in their culinary repertoire later on. This is how they develop good eating habits in the long term.

Feeding children is an adventure for child and parent. And as with any adventure, you don't necessarily know what awaits you. Babies go from surprise to surprise with each new food, and parents will discover whether they are taste adventurers or cautious explorers. You will adapt to your child's pace, and not the contrary. You will be a guide, a role model and an ally.

BIOLOGY 101

THE ORAL SKILLS OF LITTLE ONES

From birth to 6 months, babies have the oral motor skills to suckle, suck and swallow.

Around 6 months, babies can move their jaws up and down, allowing them to chew and eat certain solid foods even though they don't have teeth.

Between around 8 and 12 months, they start to control lateral tongue movements. This allows them to move food to their gums or teeth and to bite and chew a wider variety of foods.

Between 12 and 18 months, they have an easier time chewing.

Up to around 24 months, they continue to improve their oral skills.

INTRODUCING COMPLEMENTARY FOODS

Nature knows what it's doing: breast milk is the best food for babies. Up to age 6 months, it meets all of their nutritional needs (except for vitamin D, for which a supplement is recommended), and its benefits extend beyond this. Breast milk effectively protects against certain illnesses, including gastrointestinal and respiratory infections – fewer runny noses and upset tummies are nothing to sneeze at! Breastfeeding even seems to have a protective effect against children being overweight or obese. Not to mention the fact that breast milk is always ready, always tastes good, always at the right temperature and always free.

Around the age of 6 months, babies are ready to start eating food other than mother's milk or infant formula. But since every baby is unique, readiness may vary slightly from infant to infant. The official recommendation from Canada, the United Kingdom, the United States and the World Health Organization is to feed exclusively with breast milk or formula until age 6 months. For a variety of reasons, some health care professionals recommend introducing food earlier.

For premature babies, you need to take into account their corrected age. This is the age they would be if they were born at term. For example, if a baby is born 6 weeks before term, complementary food should be introduced at around 6 months plus 6 weeks.

What is important is that a few things be in place before introducing complementary food (see the box below). These are signs that babies are physically ready to eat and that they are able to communicate to help you feed them properly.

BABIES ARE READY IF:

- They can sit unaided and can lean forward without falling
- They can bring food to their mouth on their own
- They support and control their head to shake it and signal "no"
- They can push a spoon away with their hand to show that they are no longer hungry
- They show an interest in food

Before 4 months, there is no benefit to feeding babies complementary foods. In fact, the opposite is true. Their digestive and immune systems are immature, and they have a hard time coordinating their tongue and their lips. Giving babies food will not help them sleep through the night. When they are having a growth spurt, they may ask for milk more often for a few days (both day and night), but this doesn't mean that they need complementary food.

Neither is it good to wait too long after age 6 months to introduce complementary foods, because babies could be lacking certain nutrients and have a harder time accepting food flavors and consistencies.

You might start offering your baby complementary foods the day your baby turns 6 months, or two or three weeks before, or two or three days after, who knows? Observe your baby carefully. Babies will let you know when they are ready (see p. 11).

GET RID OF THE INTRODUCTION CALENDAR

Recommendations about feeding infants have changed in a number of ways in recent years. The calendar that suggested steps for introducing food was abandoned, particularly since we now know that starting at 6 months babies are ready to eat all food groups (vegetables and fruits, meat and substitutes, grains, dairy products and soy) and that it's pointless, and even contraindicated, to wait beyond this age to introduce foods that are potential allergens (see p. 28).

With the calendar gone, introducing complementary foods is more flexible. You can introduce them in any order, provided you start by serving food that is high in iron (see p. 24).

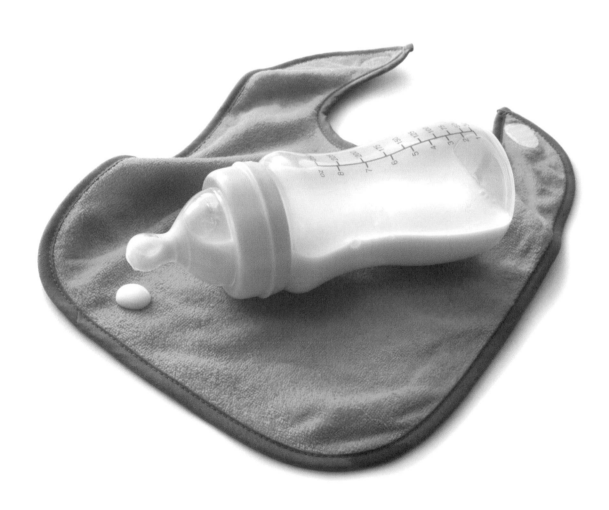

THE SPECIFIC NEEDS OF LITTLE ONES

Babies have specific nutritional needs. They are not miniature adults. The major difference between an infant and an adult can be summed up in one word: growth. Babies' rate of growth during their first year is faster than during the rest of their lives. Their body is a building site. To make sure the work goes well, they need a lot of building materials, which are provided in food.

Your baby needs a lot of energy (calories). While adults should get around 30% of their energy from fat, babies need around 50% of the calories they consume to be fat. Since their stomach is small, they can't eat large amounts of food to cover their needs. So you need to concentrate on foods that are particularly high in calories, like the calories provided by fats.

It's not just a question of calories. Fats are also essential building blocks for the brain. After fatty tissue, the brain is the fattiest organ in the body. And fats help the body absorb certain vitamins and other nutrients and go into making hormones. Babies who don't get enough fat are more at risk of being overweight in the long run. This is in part related to an imbalance in a hormone that regulates hunger. So this is why it is a good idea to serve babies fat (see *Fats*, p. 55) and to avoid foods that are low in fat.

In addition to fat, a number of nutritional elements are essential to help your baby grow and develop in good health. These are proteins, folates, vitamins B12 and D, iron, calcium, magnesium and omega-3 fatty acids (see *A Few Nutritional Elements Essential for Growth*, p. 15). These are the main growth nutrients, but not all of them. We could list all the minerals, vitamins and other known nutritional elements and assign each a number of important roles in the development of babies. Just remember that you will meet your baby's needs by serving a variety of nourishing foods. No one food provides everything a growing body needs. A varied diet will complement milk and provide a range of nutritional elements essential for babies to grow.

A FEW NUTRITIONAL ELEMENTS ESSENTIAL FOR GROWTH

Fats: for energy, to develop the brain and absorb certain vitamins

Protein: for the development and proper functioning of the muscles, the heart, the blood, the immune system and a number of other organs

Iron: for developing the brain, chemical reactions and carrying oxygen to the cells

Folates and vitamin B12: as essential as iron, for healthy blood

Calcium, magnesium and vitamin D: for growing and strengthening bones

Omega-3 fatty acids: for the development of the brain, the nervous system and the eyes. These essential fats may even have a positive effect on emotion and behavior

DEVELOPING TASTES
OR WHY BABIES DON'T LIKE THINGS ON THE FIRST TRY

There are foods that babies like right away and others that make them pull a face in disgust. They don't like everything on the first try, and that's perfectly natural. Babies are innately attracted to sweet things. This is why they instantly like mother's milk. And most babies are just as naturally wary of bitterness. Most plant poisons have a bitter taste, so this is a method of protection behind our evolution.

Liking foods is the result of learning, and your role is to help your baby learn. So it is helpful to know a little bit more about developing tastes in babies.

FROM THE MOTHER'S BELLY TO THE FIRST SPOON-FED MEALS

Before birth, through the umbilical cord and amniotic fluid, babies experience a range of oral and nasal sensations that familiarize them with their mothers' diet. This first step in taste development can influence their preferences at birth. For example, babies whose mothers ate more carrots during the final months of their pregnancy may show a preference for carrots. However, tastes and preferences evolve with experience.

Baby is born! Babies continue to get familiar with the flavor of foods their mothers eat. This time it is through breast milk, the taste of which changes every time they nurse. Infant formulas always deliver a uniform taste, and it seems that breast-fed babies more easily accept a wide variety of foods than those who are bottle fed. But again, that's not all there is to it!

Beginning at 6 months, babies have their first direct contact with different flavors. Sweet foods (like apple, pear, carrot, sweet potato and baby cereal) can be easily introduced into their food repertoire. However, bitter or acidic foods (such as grapefruit, blackberries, olives, Brussels sprouts, celery and many other vegetables) are harder to like. These preferences generally grow less intense with age, particularly if you expose your baby to a wide variety of food. Remember that children like foods that are familiar. And to be familiar, they have to see them often. Then they will be more inclined to taste them. So you have a crucial role to play in helping them accept food.

THE DIFFERENCE BETWEEN BABIES AND ADULTS

Babies detect flavors differently than adults. They have a lot more taste buds on their tongue, and they are more sensitive. As a result, their taste experiences are much more intense than ours. This is why babies sometimes react so strongly to certain flavors.

GENETICS

Every child is unique. They register flavors differently, and they have their own sensitivity threshold. Babies who are more sensitive to tastes are called hypergeusic or supertasters. They perceive flavors, including bitterness, at greater intensity. They may be "fussy" about food. On the other end of the spectrum, there are babies who perceive the taste of food less; they are hypogeusic. They tend to accept certain foods much more readily than other babies.

FOOD HABITS YOU INSTILL IN YOUR BABY

Habits influence tastes and preferences much more than genetics. Expose babies repeatedly to a variety of foods. This is how they become familiar with different flavors and textures, and how they develop their taste. They may enjoy certain foods right away or take more time. Don't force them to eat or even to try something if they don't want to.

THE FIVE SENSES

All of our senses participate in eating. Certain foods are appetizing just looking at them. We enjoy their smell, their texture and even the sound they make when broken or chewed. These are all aspects that children discover with each new food. So they may study a food from every angle before putting it in their mouths. They may look at it for a while before bringing their nose closer to smell it. Then they may venture a touch or a taste. These steps can happen in a single meal, but they can also take 15 to 20 presentations for certain foods. Sometimes this can take years. Just think about Brussels sprouts or goat cheese, which you may have taken years to enjoy.

A FEW DIFFICULTIES

When you start giving your baby food, it may not go as expected. Your baby may be less interested, slower or clumsier than you anticipated. You may also face minor difficulties or reactions that you didn't expect. Here are some situations that may cause concern, and a bit of reassurance.

BABY SPITS IT OUT

With babies' first meals, it can be hard to tell whether they have swallowed any food because there is so much on their chin and cheeks. That's to be expected. They are getting used to new textures and flavors. They are developing skills (see *Biology 101*, p. 10) and their tastes (see *Developing Tastes*, p. 16). Accept their pace of learning without scolding them. If your baby can't swallow food, even after a few weeks, talk to your doctor. A specialist may be required.

BABY VOMITS

This can happen if a baby's digestive system is immature and they are forced to eat. Vomiting can also be a symptom of a food allergy. If your child vomits when eating one food or a few foods in particular, talk to your doctor, who may order tests.

BABY RETCHES

Retching while eating is a natural reflex that protects babies from choking. It's called the gag reflex. It happens when food gets a bit too far back on their tongue and helps them bring it back to the front. This reflex is pronounced in babies before they perfect their ability to chew and swallow. It diminishes over time. If the gag reflex persists, talk to your doctor to find the cause.

BABY HAS GAS AND BLOATING

Babies have to adapt to new food. So do their intestines. And there may be new foods on the menu more likely to cause gas and bloating (such as broccoli, cauliflower, Brussels sprouts, legumes). By starting with small quantities and including these foods regularly on the menu, the discomfort subsides. Bloating can also be caused by air entering a baby's stomach while eating. Their stomach distends because it has few muscles at their age. The air is released through burping and gas.

BABY SEEMS CONSTIPATED

When babies start to eat, their stools get more solid and there are fewer of them. One stool every four days is normal for some children. Constipation occurs when stools are small and hard, or large and painful. A lack of fluids or dietary fiber may cause constipation. Stress or a change in routine can also contribute to it. See your doctor if the constipation goes on for more than one week, if there is blood in the stool, of if your child has a bad stomachache or vomits.

- Give babies more to drink. Give them as much milk as they want and give them water in a glass between drinking and eating.

- Make sure the menu contains high-fiber foods (such as fruit, vegetables, legumes and whole grains).

- You can add 1 to 3 tsp of oat bran or 1 tsp of flaxseed oil to their cereal.

- Feed them Prune Purée (see recipe p. 136).

- Don't deprive babies of cheese, bananas, rice or other foods, because they do not cause constipation.

BABY HARDLY EATS

Babies' hunger and appetite varies. It can be weaker when they have a cold, when they are teething, if they are taking medication, if they are excited or tired or when their growth slows for a while. Healthy babies eat varying amounts every day – sometimes a lot, sometimes almost nothing. This is normal. If they are growing well, don't worry.

- Give them smaller portions.

- Let them choose what order to eat their food in and how much they want.

- Take away their plate when they are no longer hungry, without commenting or scolding.

BABY IS CHUBBY

Babies are usually chubby-cheeked and plump, but this roundness generally disappears over time. Don't worry, it is not a sign that your baby will develop a weight problem. You shouldn't try to control how much food babies eat. They need to be sure that they won't be deprived and that they can continue to listen to signals of hunger and fullness.

BABY REFUSES TO USE A SPOON

If babies refuse a spoon and purées after several days of trying, they may prefer chunks and they may prefer to try to eat on their own. You can let them handle the spoon and offer them something other than purées. Give them a bit of independence (see *Let Babies Eat on Their Own (a Little!)*, p. 66) and apply a few principles of baby led weaning (see *Baby Led Weaning*, p. 32). Whatever you do, don't force them.

BABY IS PLAYING WITH FOOD

Dunking their fingers in yogurt, squishing bread through their hands, pouring soup on the high-chair tray, dumping spaghetti on their head... Babies are just having fun and getting to know food. It makes a mess and requires patience, of course, but it's beneficial for babies. But teach babies not to throw food on the floor. Wasting food should not be encouraged.

DIETARY RECOMMENDATIONS

Because babies are growing and more fragile, they have specific dietary needs. They need food that helps them grow and develop, and they should not eat food that compromises their health. Their diet has to follow steps and important principles. It's pretty easy… you'll see! First we need to talk about choices of food and how to serve it.

By following these recommendations, you help your baby develop good eating habits, and in a fun atmosphere — pleasure is the secret to lasting good habits! At around 12 months, they will eat practically like the rest of the family. Until then, there is a lot to learn and discover.

RECOMMENDATIONS:

1. Start diversifying with foods high in iron
2. Introduce other foods gradually
3. Wean gradually
4. Develop your child's tastes
5. Prevent fussy eating
6. Vary their diet: foods to serve and avoid
7. Eliminate the risk of choking
8. Serve plain food
9. Prevent food poisoning
10. Let babies eat on their own (a little!)
11. Don't camouflage food

1 START DIVERSIFYING WITH FOODS HIGH IN IRON

Why is iron so important? Because babies are born with a limited reserve of iron that dwindles over time. At around 6 months, they need food that has iron. They need large amounts to grow, and the risk of iron deficiency increases between 6 and 12 months. This can result in iron deficiency anemia, which is associated with delays in cognitive development, among other things.

Beginning at age 6 months, serve your baby foods high in iron at least twice a day, ideally three times. You can start with food your baby accepts best. Serve small amounts at first to get them used to it. With time, their appetite will grow.

Meat, poultry, fish and seafood have iron that is more easily absorbed by the body than the iron in grains, legumes, eggs or tofu. To improve the absorption of plant-based iron, it is recommended to eat a bit of meat, poultry or fish, or a fruit or vegetable high in vitamin C (such as broccoli, pepper, orange, strawberries) in the same meal.

THE BEST SOURCES OF IRON

- Enriched baby cereal
- Meat: beef, veal, lamb, pork, etc.
- Poultry: chicken, turkey, duck, etc.
- Fish and seafood: trout, sardines, shrimp, etc.
- Eggs
- Tofu, tempeh
- Legumes: lentils, edamame, black beans, etc.

2 INTRODUCE OTHER FOODS GRADUALLY

THE ORDER

Once your baby is eating foods high in iron twice a day (see Recommendation 1, p. 24), you can offer other foods in the order you like. Physically, your baby is ready to eat food from all food groups. Cow's milk is the only food that you should wait to serve until your baby is 9 months old.

Most often, people start with vegetables and fruit. Fruit is a good snack if babies aren't hungry enough to eat it at meals.

After introducing a few fruits, vegetables and meat, you can include cheese and yogurt in your baby's diet. There is no rush for dairy products, because breast milk and infant formula still form the basis of their diet (see *Vary Their Diet: Foods to Serve and Avoid*, p. 46.)

FREQUENCY OF NEW FOODS

You can introduce a new food every day, and even more often if your menu is more varied. The only new foods you should wait two to three days between serving are foods with high allergen potential, so you can spot a possible allergic reaction (see *Food Allergens*, p. 28).

Offer your baby one vegetable or fruit at a time so your baby becomes familiar with each one's unique taste. Once your baby has tasted a number of fruits or vegetables, you can mix them up.

It may take several days for them to like a food. Don't force them to eat it. If they still refuse after it has been served several times, wait a bit. Keep regularly offering them food they already know. You don't need to wait for them to like a food before having them discover others. It is important to familiarize them with a wide range of foods from an early age. Your role is to help their tastes evolve.

FOOD ALLERGENS

Delaying introducing food allergens does not prevent allergies. But there are still a few precautions you should take. To identify the food responsible for an allergic reaction, here are a few principles to follow for the main potential food allergens (see the list below). Even if these precautions don't prevent allergies, they help you quickly identify the food responsible for a problem.

THE MAIN POTENTIAL FOOD ALLERGENS

- Peanuts
- Wheat
- Fish and seafood
- Milk
- Mustard
- Nuts
- Eggs
- Sesame
- Soy
- Food containing sulfites

Here are the signs that your child may be having an allergic reaction. See a doctor right away if you see any of the following symptoms after introducing a new food.

- Their lips or tongue swell

- They have difficulty breathing

- They vomit

- They suddenly become irritable or drowsy, or their general condition changes suddenly and significantly

- Red patches or spots appear on their body

- There is swelling around the eyes

- Their nose is runny and itchy

PRECAUTIONS

- Introduce foods with allergen potential one at a time

- Start with a small quantity, for example 1 tsp, and increase gradually

- When babies eat a food for the first time, serve it cooked. Cooking reduces the allergen effect of foods (particularly fruits and vegetables)

- Wait at least two or three days between introducing two foods that are potential allergens

- Make sure babies are exposed to the variety of food that the family eats before age one

Start meals with small portions. During the first few days, some babies eat barely one or two spoonfuls of cereal or purée, and they have more on their chin than in their belly. Serve them more if they show you they are still hungry. Gradually increase the size of portions by adjusting them to the needs your baby expresses. Portions the size of their fist are a good start.

The amount of food babies eat at each meal or as a snack will vary depending on how hungry they are, the time of day, their fatigue, the amount of milk they have had and how much they like the food being served. They are the ones who decide, because they are the only ones who know how much meets their needs (see *Biology 101*, p. 10).

Smooth purée is often the first step in solid foods, but it is not mandatory. The first purées can have a coarse texture and even contain chunks. Regardless of your baby's starting point, be sure to serve food with a lumpy texture no later than 9 months of age to get her used to chewing so she doesn't get lazy.

The consistency of baby cereal, meat and substitutes, fruit and vegetables are normally offered in the following order:

1. Smooth purée

2. Coarser or thicker purée

3. Lumpy purée

4. Soft pieces and grated food

5. Small chunks

By spending a maximum of one month on each of these steps, babies go from smooth purée to lumpy purée by the age of 9 months at the latest, as recommended. The evolution can happen at a similar pace afterward, aiming to have the foods from your meal cut into small pieces at the age of 12 months. Give children a chance to evolve gradually. Watch them and listen to them to adapt their diet to their ability to chew and swallow. Don't stay at the same stage of consistency for no reason. Offering babies different textures helps them develop their oral motor skills.

Dry, crunchy food or food that melts easily in the mouth (such as dry cereal, crackers and biscuits for babies, bread crusts, toast) are added alongside the above steps. Beginning at age 6 months, babies are able to eat them. However, to prevent choking, avoid certain shapes and textures of foods before they are 4 years old (see *Eliminate the Risk of Choking*, p. 59).

BABY LED WEANING

Baby led weaning involves introducing solid food, in different sized pieces, and not a purée. Babies take the pieces of food themselves to bring them to their mouths. They are generally served food from the family menu, provided it is appropriate.

Baby led weaning is not for all babies. Some take longer than others to develop the motor skills to feed themselves on their own. If that is the case, the risk with this type of diet is that they don't eat enough and so don't gain enough weight.

You can apply the principles of baby led weaning flexibly. For example, give babies cereal enriched with iron, and even other purées from time to time, while offering them whole foods or food in pieces at each meal. Being flexible allows you to reap the benefits of the method while minimizing the inconveniences: it's the best of both worlds.

- Food is introduced when babies can sit up on their own and manipulate food, in short, when they are ready to eat: it's hard to go wrong. So there is very little risk of introducing food too quickly.

- Since babies eat food from the family menu, they eat with the family. This is beneficial socially and psychologically, not to mention that parents become models for behavior.

- Babies eat at their own pace, respecting signs of hunger and satiety.

- Babies develop fine motor skills and independence.

INCONVENIENCES AND PRECAUTIONS

- Some foods on the family menu are not appropriate for babies: certain cuts of meat; very sweet, salty, spicy or fried dishes or food; as well as certain foods that are choking hazards. So you need to regularly have foods just for baby.

- When babies are making their first attempts, they do not bring food to their mouth, but they try. So it is a good idea to have something on hand to clean up little messes.

- Babies eating on their own makes mealtime longer. This can cause stress when you don't have time to stay at the table.

- If babies don't eat iron-enriched cereals (because they don't like purée) and they have a hard time eating meat, their iron intake may be a concern.

During the first week, offer food two or three times a day to get babies used to this new part of their life. They may only eat a few spoonfuls at first. The amount of food and number of meals will increase little by little.

- **From 7 to 8 months,** offer babies two or three meals, and one or two snacks per day. They will decide when and how much. Watch for any signs of hunger.

- **From 9 to 11 months,** three meals and two or three snacks are appropriate, depending on how hungry they are. They are the ones who decide on the schedule, because when babies are hungry, you feed them! Their schedule of meals and snacks varies according to their hunger and when they wake up in the morning, go to bed and have naps. It is a good idea if they have at least a few opportunities to eat with you, if they can't all the time.

- **Starting at 12 months,** set a regular schedule for meals and snacks, ideally so they can eat meals with you. With three meals and two or three snacks, you teach them to regulate their food intake. Between meals and snacks, they may be hungry, but opportunities to eat are frequent enough so they are never too hungry.

The following menus are examples (see p. 36). Babies may eat at different times of the day. At the beginning, they will probably eat small amounts. Increase portion size based on how hungry they are. Offer them liquids whenever they ask for them. If they aren't hungry enough to eat fruit after a meal, serve them fruit as a snack. Up to around 7 months, offer them breast milk with solid food during meals. Beginning at 7 months or when their appetite means that they can eat more, give them breast milk after solid food.

DON'T FORGET TO GIVE BABIES ENOUGH TO DRINK

When babies start to eat, the amount of liquid they ingest diminishes because their little stomachs get too full. Offer them something to drink regularly so that they are properly hydrated. Don't wait for them to ask, because they have a harder time expressing their thirst than their hunger – this is not a concern as long as they are breast feeding or having bottles on a regular schedule, but once you start to wean them, it is important to remember. So offer them four small glasses of milk or soy beverage (but not before 9 months) spread out between meals and snacks, and add a little glass of water in the morning, the afternoon and the evening, but don't force them to drink it.

	6 MONTHS	7 MONTHS	8 MONTHS	9 TO 11 MONTHS
Upon waking	Breast milk*	Breast milk	Breast milk	Breast milk
7 am	Breast milk Iron-enriched baby cereal	Iron-enriched baby cereal Breast milk	Iron-enriched baby cereal Fruit Breast milk	Iron-enriched baby cereal Fruit Breast milk
9 am			If baby is hungry: snack (p. 80)	Fruit
11:30 am	Breast milk	Meat or substitutes Vegetable Breast milk	Meat or substitutes Vegetable Breast milk	Meat or substitutes Cereal Vegetable Fruit Breast milk
3 pm			Unsweetened oat cereal loops or other cereal product or fruit	Cereal or fruit Dairy product, depending on appetite Water
5 pm	Breast milk Iron-enriched baby cereal	Iron-enriched baby cereal Fruit Breast milk	Iron-enriched baby cereal or meat or substitute Vegetable Fruit Breast milk	Meat or substitutes Cereal Fruit and/or plain yogurt Breast milk
7 pm	Breast milk	Breast milk	Breast milk	Breast milk

* The term "breast milk" is used to simplify the table. If babies are not breast fed, use infant formula instead (or cow's milk starting at age 9 months, if and only if babies have a good appetite for a wide variety of foods). Give them milk only when they ask.

Experts suggest introducing complementary food at around age 6 months and recommend never doing it before age 4 months.

FREQUENCY OF MEALS AND SNACKS

- The recommendations are for three meals (morning, noon and evening) and two or three snacks (in the morning, in the afternoon and in the evening if needed). The thinking is that babies have small stomachs, and it is better for them to have several opportunities to eat during the day and the evening to meet their needs. It is also better to avoid babies being hungry for too long and then eating until they feel stuffed. Snacks allow babies and children to be moderately hungry at mealtime, and to eat until they feel sated (rather than too full).

FIRST TEXTURES

- Liquid cereals are not recommended. What is recommended instead is a fairly liquid texture of purée to be spooned into your baby's mouth that is thick enough for them to not just suck it in. At age 6 months their oral motor skills allow for this.

LEGUMES

- It is suggested that lentils, beans, chickpeas, etc., become part of babies' diet starting at 6 months. By starting with small quantities, babies (and their intestines) gradually get used to them.

3 WEAN GRADUALLY

Breast milk or infant formula remains the priority during a baby's first year. This is why other foods are called "complementary." At 6 months, when babies start to eat, they will continue to drink about the same amount of milk. Starting at 7 months, you can start meals with food and finish them with milk (the amount will diminish gradually starting at 8 or 9 months).

DAILY RECOMMENDED AMOUNTS FOR BABIES

Give them milk or formula when they ask for it. They will drink around:
- 1 to 4 months: between 2 to 3 cups (500 to 750 ml) of milk*
- 4 to 8 months: between 3 to 3½ cups (750 to 875 ml) of milk*
- 9 months to 2 years: between 2½ to 3 cups (625 to 750 ml) of milk

* breast milk or infant formula

Wait until babies are between 9 and 12 months before offering them cow's milk, and limit the amount to a maximum of 3 cups (750 ml) per day, as for breast milk and infant formula. Milk should not compromise variety and should not replace other nourishing foods. And drinking too much cow's milk can cause an iron deficiency (anemia).

Breast milk: It is a good idea to breast feed exclusively until around 6 months and then in combination with foods up to one year and beyond. When the time comes, reduce one feed at a time, and wait a few days before cutting out another one. Keep the feeds that babies like most for longer and the ones that best suit your schedule.

Infant formula: If your baby drinks from a bottle, it is a good idea to start the transition to a glass at around 9 months. That said, up until one year, the main thing is that they drink milk suitable for their age, whether from a bottle or a glass. The content is more important that what it is delivered in. However, weaning from the bottle at around 9 months helps prevent cavities, because drinking from bottles leaves milk in the mouth and therefore in contact with the teeth longer. Even if the sugar in milk is natural, it feeds bacteria that cause cavities.

4 DEVELOP YOUR CHILD'S TASTES

Repeated: Keep offering your child food even if it has been pushed away several times. Serve it regularly, for example once a month. Don't go overboard and serve it too often.

Positive: The setting for a meal should be warm and positive. Children tend to associate food with emotions they are experiencing when they discover them. If they are happy and in a good mood, they will remember the food fondly and will want to eat it again more than if they are upset. Don't force babies to taste or eat foods. This creates tension, and meals become negative experiences. Babies may finally decide to eat just to obey, but they won't take any pleasure in it. It will be counter-productive and nobody wins.

Exposure: To get to know food, children need to see it on their plate. Serve them a small amount to begin with to avoid discouraging them or having it wasted.

STICK TO ONE FORM OF PRESENTATION

For babies, carrot purée and carrots in matchsticks seem like two different foods. To help them get familiar with a food, serve it the same way until they accept it. Otherwise, it's a bit like starting over with each new presentation. That said, it is possible that by trying different ways of presenting food, you will find one they like. It's worth a try.

OFFER A NEW FOOD WITH FOOD THEY ALREADY LIKE

For babies, an unfamiliar food on their plate can be a source of concern. Be sure to serve them at least one food they like at the same time. It is reassuring for them, because if they don't like the new food, they can still eat. Plus, babies will start with a positive opinion about at least one thing on their plate, which serves the cause of the entire meal!

ENCOURAGE BABIES, BUT DON'T FORCE THEM

You can encourage children to try something by saying, for example: "I think you're going to like this," "you can just try a little taste and put it back on your plate if you don't like it" or "good for you for trying it." Avoid putting any pressure on them or congratulating them about the amount of food eaten. Don't say "way to go, you ate it all up" or "just two more mouthfuls and then you're done." Particularly avoid saying things that make children think you are proud of them when they eat more. Respecting their tastes and the pace at which they develop them is the best way not to create feelings of revulsion or systematic defiance. If they refuse a food, don't force them. Serve it to them again a few days later.

AVOID REWARD SYSTEMS

Do not negotiate to convince babies to eat food they don't like, for example, by promising them a toy if they eat their vegetables or withdrawing a privilege if they don't. These practices just make the rejected food even less appealing, because it is seen as an obstacle to a gift.

SHOW THEM IT'S GOOD

Babies learn through imitation, and generally you are the one they imitate. They will more readily agree to try a new food if they see you enjoying it.

TALK TO THEM ABOUT FOOD

Describe the food you are serving and be enthusiastic: "wow, these carrots are a pretty orange," "mmm, this fish smells good," "look at how long and thin this asparagus is," and so forth. Discovering food opens up a world of pleasure for children. You help them become aware of it when you talk up the food. Describing a food's characteristics goes a long way towards familiarizing your child with it.

MAKE THEM A PLACE IN THE KITCHEN

Babies are too small to cook. But they can watch. Pull up a highchair up so your child can watch you work. Get your child to smell or touch the food. This is another way for them to get familiar with it.

BE A ROLE MODEL AT THE TABLE

The social aspect of eating is another important reason your baby should be part of family meals. If your meal schedule doesn't suit your baby's, make a place for baby at the table even if it's not time to eat. Whether or not they share your meal, it is a good opportunity to get them familiar with food, to create reference points and to shape their habits and meal preferences. Television, tablets and smartphones have no place at the table. Not only do they prevent people from paying attention to others and to food, they also prevent people from feeling the signs of hunger and fullness.

5 PREVENT FUSSY EATING

Babies who don't like a food the first time or even after a few tries are not fussy eaters. They are normal children who are developing their tastes. How you react to their refusal determines whether they develop fussy behavior.

DON'T MAKE MEALS JUST FOR BABIES

If you make another dish because your child doesn't like what is being served, you are reinforcing the refusal and lowering the chances of your child liking the food one day. Not to mention that you encourage children to take that way out the minute they have the slightest hesitation about food.

DON'T OFFER THEM A SNACK RIGHT AFTER THE MEAL

Don't give children a snack right after the meal, because this is another easy way out for children who don't want to try a new food.

RESPECT THEIR SIGNALS OF HUNGER AND FULLNESS

From birth, you offer babies a breast or bottle on demand when they are hungry. You let them decide when to stop eating. Babies instinctively know how to meet their needs, and you listen without questioning. The same should apply when it comes to introducing complementary food. Let babies decide how much they want to eat.

DON'T BUY "CHILDREN'S" FOOD

Get children used to eating the same food as the entire family. They don't need colorful characters, fun shapes or huge doses of sugar to enjoy food. They learn to like what you eat together during a meal. If you offer them products for children too often they'll get used to them, enjoy them and look for them. Children will be perfectly open to ordinary food.

DON'T ANSWER FOR THEM

Whether you are at a friend's, with family or at a restaurant, other people often offer children food. Someone may offer them food they have never tried or liked. Let them decide if they want to taste it or not and, most importantly, avoid saying that they don't like it. You never know when the change will happen. Sometimes all it takes is a specific context or a new person to encourage children to taste food they have rejected in the past.

6 VARY THEIR DIET: FOODS TO SERVE AND AVOID

Every fruit, vegetable, grain, meat or substitute — in short, every different food — offers different nutrients in varying amounts. So by serving babies a varied menu, they get everything they need to grow up in good health.

In this section, portions are provided for information. They may vary among babies. Let your baby decide how much to eat.

CEREAL

PURÉED CEREALS

Serve: Enriched baby cereal

- First offer "starter" or "beginner" store-bought cereal. Start with cereal that contains a single sort of grain, for example barley, oats or rice before introducing mixed cereal. Choose those you add breast milk or infant formula to. They will be better for babies than those with (cow's) milk powder.

- Beginning at 8 months, you can offer "stage 2" cereal, but you don't have to, because aside from the variety of flavors, they offer nothing more. In fact, they tend to have unnecessary ingredients and more sugar. Keep serving the plainest cereal possible. It is easy to add your own puréed fruit or chunks of fruit to mix up the flavor.

- The best cereals are those that don't contain sugar. Note that the oligofructose that you see on some lists of ingredients is not added sugar, but a sort of dietary fiber that feeds good bacteria in babies' intestines.

- Choose cereals that meet 100% of the daily iron requirements for babies in each 28 g serving. Check the nutritional value table. This is the daily value percentage indicated by "% DV."

Avoid: Brown rice cereal

It can contain worrisome levels of arsenic. White rice cereal is acceptable as part of a varied diet.

How to serve it: Start with a thin purée, but not too liquidy either. Gradually thicken as you go.

Amount: Start with 1 tsp dried cereal combined with breast milk (or infant formula). Offer babies more if they accept it and then gradually increase the amount over time according to how hungry they are. One portion equals around ⅓ cup (80 ml) of dried cereal.

Up to 2 years old: Keep serving iron-enriched baby cereal on the menu until children are two years old. They may not want to eat it as purée up to that age, but you can use it to make cookies, muffins, pancakes and crêpes, for example (see recipe section, p. 105).

CEREAL (CONTINUED)

READY-TO-EAT CEREAL FOR BABIES

Ready-to-eat cereal for babies (like loops) is generally much lower in iron than puréed cereal, so it doesn't replace it. But you can offer it occasionally as a snack. It allows babies to try out new food textures and develop their dexterity, because they pick it up with their little fingers. Choose unsweetened cereal, like small oat loops. Avoid colored loops or other cereal like that.

OTHER GRAIN PRODUCTS

Serve: Bread crust, toast, pita bread, naan bread, tortilla, pasta, millet, quinoa, couscous, oatmeal, bread sticks, salt-free crackers, short-grain rice, crêpes

- You can introduce this food once babies are eating food high in iron at least twice a day.

- Choose whole-grain products at least every other time.

Warning: Babies can choke on rice. Start with short-grain rice (risotto or sushi rice) mashed with a fork.

How to serve it:

- As needed, first mash pasta, couscous, rice, quinoa and millet with a fork or cut it into small pieces, then serve in its regular form once your baby is ready.

- Offer bread crusts and different kinds of bread, crackers and bread sticks so babies can grasp them themselves.

Amount: Serve a portion around the size of your baby's fist and then offer more if your baby is still hungry.

FOODS HIGH IN PROTEIN: MEAT AND SUBSTITUTES

MEAT AND POULTRY

Serve: Lamb, chicken, turkey, veal, beef, pork, liver

Avoid: Ham, salami, sausages, bacon and other deli meat

These foods contain too much salt, fat, nitrates and nitrites. Nitrates and nitrites are transformed into potential carcinogens in the body.

FISH

Serve: Alaska salmon, Pacific halibut, sole, turbot, tilapia, striped bass, white-fish, salmon trout and other trout (except lake trout), Arctic char, smelt

- If you use canned fish, make sure it has no added salt.
- You can leave bones in some fish like salmon, because they are soft. If you mash them well with a fork, babies can eat them with no trouble.

Avoid: Swordfish, shark, bass, pike, walleye, muskie, marlin, monkfish, lake trout, red or white tuna

- These fish can contain pollutants and heavy metals.
- Avoid sushi and other raw or cold-smoked fish, because they can harbor bacteria that are harmful to babies.

How to serve it: Fish needs to be thoroughly cooked. Serve fish first as a smooth purée. Gradually modify the texture at a pace suited to your baby: less-smooth purée, then finely chopped food and, finally, small tender pieces.

Amount: Start with 1 tsp. Gradually increase to 4 to 6 tbsp a day at around 12 months.

Serve: Egg yolk, then whole egg

Start with egg yolk if babies eat just a little. The iron and fat are concentrated in the yolk. Serve the whole egg once their appetite increases.

Avoid: Raw or undercooked eggs

They can harbor bacteria that are harmful to babies.

How to serve them: Serve them fully cooked, first as a smooth purée, which is easy to do with a fork, adding a bit of milk or infant formula. Gradually move to lumpy purée, mashed eggs and then small pieces.

Amount: Start with 1 tsp of egg yolk. Gradually increase to the entire yolk, then the whole egg (yolk and white). At around 12 months, babies will eat an egg or two in one sitting.

Serve: Any type of lentils, dried beans, chickpeas, tempeh, regular tofu and silken tofu.

Silken tofu is lower in protein and iron. It cannot be the only source of protein in a meal.

Avoid: Tofu dessert to start

Tofu dessert has too much sugar. Start with plain tofu.

How to serve them: Serve legumes as a smooth purée or simply mashed with a fork. You can cook them yourself or use canned legumes thoroughly rinsed.

Regular tofu can be crumbled or diced. Just heat it up; it doesn't need to be cooked. Silken tofu has the texture of custard and babies can eat it as is.

Tempeh can be crumbled or diced, just like tofu, but it needs to be cooked.

Amount: Start with 1 to 2 tsp of legumes so babies' intestines get used to foods that can cause gas. Gradually increase to 2 to 4 tbsp per meal. A portion of tofu is around 1 oz (30 g).

VEGETARIAN BABIES

Babies can have a vegetarian diet and grow up healthy provided their diet is balanced, varied and concentrated in energy (calories). Otherwise, they may have nutritional deficiencies or growth or developmental delays. It is a good idea to consult a nutritionist to ensure children are getting all the nutrients they need.

VEGETABLES

Serve: All vegetables

- Start with orange or yellow vegetables, which are mild (e.g., squash, carrots, sweet potatoes, corn, red, orange or yellow pepper).

- Then add green vegetables (e.g., peas, green beans, zucchini, asparagus, avocados).

- Finally, serve the rest (e.g., broccoli, cauliflower, eggplant, tomatoes, mushrooms, turnip, potatoes, parsnips, etc.).

How to serve them:
- You can start with smooth or slightly chunky purées depending on your baby's ability. Gradually move to cooked vegetables cut in small or larger pieces (around the size of baby's fist) for your baby to chew on.

- You can use fresh or frozen vegetables. If you use canned vegetables, make sure they have no added salt.

Amount: Start with 1 to 2 tsp when serving a vegetable for the first time. If your baby doesn't like it, there will be less waste. A portion is around the size of your baby's fist.

FRUIT

Serve: All fruit

Start with any fruit you can purée or mash with a fork. Once babies adapt to new textures, continue with citrus (clementines, oranges, grapefruit), removing the membrane over each section. Wait until age 9 or 12 months before offering babies cut grapes.

Avoid or limit: Fruit juice

It is less nourishing than fruit and increases the risk of cavities. Babies don't need it. If you want to give it to them anyway, make it half juice (with no sugar added) and half water, and don't give them more than 1/4 cup (60 ml) a day.

How to serve it:
- You can start with smooth or slightly chunky purées. A great deal of ripe, tender fruit (e.g., bananas, cantaloupe, pineapple, watermelon) can simply be mashed with a fork or puréed in a blender without cooking. For others (e.g., apples, peaches, pears, apricots, nectarines, plums), it is better to cook them before puréeing. Ripe berries such as blueberries, raspberries and strawberries can be served raw or cooked. You can press berries through a strainer to remove the seeds if you want to.

- You can serve babies raw or grated fruit or fruit in pieces.

- Choose fresh or frozen fruit. You can also serve homemade or store-bought (no sugar added) fruit sauce or canned sauce (in juice and not syrup).

Amount: Serve a portion the size of your baby's fist. Don't force your baby to eat everything, and just serve more if your baby is still hungry.

DAIRY AND SOY PRODUCTS

There is no rush for dairy products, because babies are still drinking breast milk (or infant formula). Once they are eating food high in iron at least twice a day, you can start including dairy on the menu.

Serve: Yogurt (4% to 10% M.F.), kefir, cheese or soy cheese, soy beverage (not before 9 months)

Avoid: Cow's milk and unpasteurized cheese

- Do not serve babies cow's milk before 9 months, because it can reduce their appetite for other food and reduce their iron intake. Wait until at least 9 months (ideally 12 months) and until they are eating a variety of iron-rich foods before adding it to the menu. When they are ready, serve them pasteurized 3.25% milk. Don't give them more than 3 cups (750 ml) per day.

- Avoid unpasteurized cheese, because it can contain bacteria that are harmful to babies.

How to serve them:
- Plain yogurt.

  Fat yogurt is creamy, and its flavor is mellower than low-fat plain yogurt. Your baby will learn to like it as is. Then you can mix it with a bit of fruit sauce.

- Mild firm cheese (e.g., Cheddar, mozzarella) or other firm cheese your family eats: grated or in thin slices.

- Fresh or ricotta cheese: as is, by the spoonful

- Soy beverage: enriched (fortified), unflavored and not low fat. Plant-based drinks (rice, almond, oat and hemp) are not nourishing enough to replace milk.

Amount: Start with 2 or 3 tbsp yogurt or cheese, then increase according to your baby's appetite. At around 12 months, a portion is around ⅓ cup (80 ml) of yogurt or 1 oz (30 g) of cheese.

FATS

To satisfy babies' need for fat, you do not need to add butter or oil to everything they eat. Just be sure to include food in their diet that is both fat and nourishing, rather than nutritionally poor fat.

Serve:
- Breast milk (or infant formula)
- Whole milk (not before 9 months)
- Cheese
- Whole-milk yogurt
- Eggs
- Fatty fish (salmon, trout, Arctic char, mackerel, etc.)
- Meat and poultry
- Peanut butter and other nut butters
- Avocado

Avoid:
- Chips
- Deli meats
- Fries
- Pastry
- Diet products

WATER

Up to age 6 months, breast milk satisfies babies' thirst. It contains more water at the beginning of a feed then becomes richer in protein and fat as the feed goes on. So if babies seem thirsty on hot days, you can breast feed more often.

In principle, infant formula diluted according to the manufacturer's instructions also satisfies babies' thirst. But if it is very hot out, your baby has a fever or is sick and your baby's appetite for milk is suppressed, you can offer water by spoon or glass to prevent dehydration.

If babies are less than 4 months old, boil the water at a rolling boil for at least one minute, regardless of whether it comes from the tap (including aqueducts and private wells) or is bottled, whether for drinking or diluting infant formula. You can keep it in the refrigerator in a carefully washed or sterilized container for up to three days or for 24 hours at room temperature away from the sun's rays.

If babies are older than 4 months, you no longer need to boil the water. When babies start to eat, regularly offer them a bit of water in a glass.

Water that's right for babies (boiled before age 4 months):

- Tap water

- Water from private wells that has been tested twice a year

- Bottled spring water

Water that's not right for babies:

- Water from a lake or natural source that has not been regularly tested

- Bottled mineral water

- Sparkling water

- Warm tap water (because it can contain more lead, copper and bacteria than cold water)

WARNING

Do not use household water filtering or treatment systems until your baby is 6 months old. We don't know whether water softeners installed on taps, reverse osmosis devices or charcoal filters are effective and, more importantly, safe.

HONEY

One food babies are not ready to eat is honey. It could make them sick, because it can contain spores of the *Clostridium botulinum* bacteria. If they are ingested, these spores develop in infant intestines and produce a poison that causes botulism. This extremely serious illness causes generalized weakness, which even limits crying and the suckling reflex. Other symptoms are irritability, loss of head control, constipation and, in some cases, paralysis of the diaphragm that makes breathing difficult.

A small percentage of honeys contain *Clostridium botulinum* spores: around 5% in Canada. But since the risk exists and the consequences are dramatic, avoid feeding babies honey until they are 12 months old. This applies to any honey, whether pasteurized or not, because the heat from pasteurization does not destroy the spores. For the same reason, baked goods made with honey should be avoided.

7 ELIMINATE THE RISK OF CHOKING

Babies gradually improve their ability to chew and swallow, but it is not perfected until they are a few years old. You should avoid giving them food that is small, hard, round, smooth or sticky until age 4, because it is hard to chew and can easily obstruct the respiratory tract.

TIPS FOR ELIMINATING THE RISK OF CHOKING

- Always stay near babies while they eat.

- Seat babies comfortably before feeding them.

- Teach babies to take small bites and chew thoroughly.

- Don't allow children to walk, run, jump, dance or swing with food in their mouths.

- Find out about first aid for children in case of choking.

- See the table on p. 60 and 61.

TYPE OF FOOD	DANGER	PRECAUTIONS
Nuts, peanuts, seeds	Whole Crunchy nut butter Nut butter by the spoonful (because the thick texture can cause suffocation)	Spread a thin layer on toast
Bread	Soft part of fresh bread (once it comes in contact with saliva, it becomes hard and compact)	Serve only crust, toast, flatbread (e.g., pita, tortilla, naan, chapatti)
Hard vegetables (e.g., carrots, celery, turnip, cauliflower, etc.)	Raw	• Up to 1 year: cook until soft and then purée, cut in strips or large pieces • Up to 2 years: grate • Up to 4 years: blanch (boil for 2 or 3 minutes) and remove strings from celery and snow peas
Soft vegetables (e.g., cucumber, mushrooms, tomatoes, peppers)	Whole or in large pieces	Up to 2 years: cut in strips or thin slices
Leafy vegetables (e.g., lettuce)	Whole leaves or in large pieces (because they can stick in the throat)	Up to 2 years: cut or chop
Apples	Whole	Peel and core • Up to 1 year: cook to purée or grate raw • Up to 2 years: cut in pieces

TYPE OF FOOD	DANGER	PRECAUTIONS
Peaches, pears	Whole	Remove peach pit Up to 2 years: peel

Fresh grapes	Whole	• Up to 1 year:
		  cut in quarters
		
		• Up to 4 years:
		  cut in half

Blueberries, raspberries, strawberries, blackberries	Whole	• Up to 1 year: press
		  through a strainer to
		  remove small seeds
		
		• Up to 2 years: cut in
		  small pieces

Dried fruit (e.g., raisins, dried apricots, dried cranberries)	Whole	Finely chop or add to preparations (e.g., muffins) in which they are rehydrated
String cheese	Whole sticks	Strings peeled along the length
Chicken	With skin or small bones	Remove skin and be sure not to leave any small bones
Fish	With bones	Be sure to remove bones or mash them if they are soft (e.g., canned salmon)
Popcorn	All	Do not serve
Hard or sticky candies, chewing gum, throat lozenges	All	Do not serve
Ice cubes	All	Do not serve

8 SERVE PLAIN FOOD

Don't add salt or sugar to food served to babies for a number of reasons:

- Babies should discover and learn to like the natural flavor of food.

- Babies don't need salt or sugar.

- Adding salt or sugar encourages babies to like and even prefer sweet or salty food. It is better not to make this a habit.

SALT

It is recommended to wait until babies are 12 months old before giving them food with added salt. Limit the amount of salt added to family food when you want to share it with babies to reduce their consumption to a minimum. Pay particular attention to store-bought foods.

Salt is a major concern for health care professionals, because the vast majority of people eat too much of it. In the long term, too much salt is associated with kidney problems, hypertension and osteoporosis. People who eat salty foods also tend to drink more sugary drinks, which can contribute to weight problems. While this is not a concern for babies, the food choices we make for babies influence their diet in the long term.

It is important to let babies enjoy foods without salt. Eventually you can season their food with herbs, spices and other seasonings, but it is always a good idea to go easy on the salt (in cooking and at the table) and to limit processed foods, because they are the main source of it.

While too much salt is bad, a minimum is needed for good health. The sodium and chlorine contained in salt (scientifically called sodium chloride) play important roles. For example, sodium contributes to the transmission of information (nerve impulses) between the brain and the rest of the body, and enables the muscles to contract. Chlorine helps balance liquids inside and outside cells, contributes to the body's acid-base balance and promotes the transit of different substances in the blood.

SUGAR

It is a good idea to limit foods that contain added sugar. Choose plain yogurt, unsweetened cereal and fruit compotes and purées without sugar. However, recipes for homemade muffins and cookies may contain a bit of sugar. Reduce the quantities in the original recipes and try recipes naturally sweetened (in whole or in part) with date purée, apple compote or banana purée, for example.

HERBS AND SPICES

To allow babies to discover plain foods, avoid adding spices or herbs when you are introducing something new. Once they have tried the food plain, you can add a few herbs and a bit of spice to get them to discover food served another way and gradually come closer to your family's menu. Go easy on the spicy food.

CHEESE

When babies start to eat cheese, you can occasionally add it to vegetable or meat purées.

9 PREVENT FOOD POISONING

Babies are vulnerable to food-borne infections, because they are not yet able to defend themselves against bacteria. Their immune system is immature and their stomachs produce little gastric acid, two defense mechanisms that will develop over time.

Symptoms of food-borne infections can include retching, vomiting, stomach cramps (stomachache), diarrhea and fever.

TIPS FOR PREVENTING FOOD POISONING

- Don't give children foods to avoid up to age 5 (see p. 65).

- Wash your hands carefully before cooking and feeding your baby, as well as after changing diapers, touching an animal, wiping noses, taking public transit, etc.

- Carefully clean work surfaces and tools before cooking.

- Use different boards, plates and utensils (or thoroughly washed in soapy warm water) for raw food (meat, poultry and fish) and cooked food. Anything that has touched raw food should not come into contact with cooked food.

- Fully cook meat, poultry, fish and eggs.

- Don't leave perishables (e.g., purée, dairy products) at room temperature. Quickly refrigerate or freeze food after purchase or preparation (if you prepare purée or meals in advance, for example).

- Change dishcloths and dishtowels every day, because they carry a lot of bacteria.

- Rinse fruit and vegetables under cold water before serving or cooking them for babies. Many hands (not always clean ones) have handled them before you.

• Unpasteurized milk and cheese

• Raw eggs and products that contain them (e.g., mayonnaise, homemade eggnog, uncooked cookie and cake batter)

• Raw or undercooked meat, poultry, fish and seafood (e.g., tartare, sushi)

• Raw sprouts (or shoots) (e.g. bean sprouts)

• Unpasteurized juice

10 LET BABIES EAT ON THEIR OWN (A LITTLE!)

Starting at 6 months, offer babies foods they can pick up with their fingers and get to their mouths on their own (e.g., bread crust, pieces of toast, soft vegetables, soft ripe fruit, grated cheese, dry cereal). This encourages them to eat on their own early on and ultimately promotes their autonomy, as well as their oral and motor skills. They can eat only small amounts of food, but this is rounded out by a diet that includes a variety of textures, such as purées.

You can offer them a spoon before they are a year old, but don't expect them to master the art for a few months. Children acquire this motor skill at around age 2. They can handle forks at around age 3.

Letting children eat a little on their own raises a few challenges.

Time. It takes longer than feeding babies with a spoon, but it's important for their development. Take the time to let them experiment.

Messes. Messes are part of experimentation and the learning process. Babies need practice to coordinate their movements, particularly when using utensils. Be patient and understanding.

Waste. To reduce waste, start by serving babies small portions. Give them more if they are still hungry.

Some babies refuse food on a spoon. They want to do everything themselves. If this is the case for your child, don't worry. They can feed themselves with pieces of soft food that they can pick up with their fingers (see *Baby Led Weaning*, p. 32).

DRINKING FROM A GLASS

Serve babies something to drink in a glass or an open cup when they are not breast or bottle feeding. Cups with a lip (or anti-spill system) don't allow babies to develop their drinking skills, because they have to suck.

At first, you will have to hold the glass or cup to their mouth. They will try to suck the liquid, and then they will develop a sucking action holding their jaw in an open, stable position. Over time they will be able to control their breathing and swallow at their own pace, and hold the glass or cup.

11 DON'T CAMOUFLAGE FOOD

When babies don't like a food after a few tries, you may be tempted to trick them by hiding the food in a purée or dish they like. It's tempting, but it's not the answer. Babies will eat the food they normally refuse without realizing it. But they won't become familiar with it and learn to like it. So this is counterproductive when it comes to developing tastes.

You don't want to have to prepare meals in secret for years, do you? And you want your children to eat a variety of foods once they decide for themselves, right? So don't camouflage food! Be patient and use the tips in *Develop Your Child's Tastes*, p. 41.

You should also avoid camouflaging the taste of food by smothering it in ketchup. First of all, children don't learn to like foods that way. Second of all, they don't need such sweet and salty condiments or sauces.

That said, including fruit, vegetable and legume purées from time to time in recipes isn't always camouflaging. You may simply want to increase the nutritional value of certain dishes, and that's just fine. Purées add vitamins, minerals and dietary fiber to meatballs, macaroni and cheese, muffins and homemade cookies. They also allow you to reduce the amount of fat and sugar used to prepare these dishes.

You just can't beat homemade purées prepared with love and fresh ingredients.

They are nutritious. Freshly prepared homemade purées are the most nutritious food available. And they haven't undergone intense heat processing like store-bought ones. Not to mention that you control the ingredients, particularly in terms of quality.

They are fast and easy to prepare. Purées have few ingredients and involve little preparation.

They are economical. You can make them using seasonal fruits and vegetables that are on sale, inexpensive cuts of meat, and legumes and tofu, which are generally affordable. You can use food you are already preparing for the family, so you don't need to buy anything extra.

They are environmentally friendly. You only use the part and amount you need, so there is very little waste. And you aren't buying one-use jars.

They are delicious. Homemade purées are like the food they are made with, both in terms of color and flavor.

They are versatile. There are as many possibilities for purées as there are vegetables and fruits at the market (or in your garden), not to mention all the possible combinations.

You can vary textures. You can gradually change the texture to adapt to your baby's chewing skills.

You can make purées for babies as you make meals, but it is more practical to make and freeze extra. That way you can make your baby's meal in no time and take food with you when you're on the go. You can also take advantage of discounts and the top freshness of some fruits and vegetables, because you make them when they are in season (even if your baby is too young to eat them), freeze them and pull them out weeks or months later.

Fresh or frozen. Choose fresh products whenever possible (fruit, vegetables, meat, poultry, fish and eggs). Seasonal fruits and vegetables are best. Cook meat, poultry and fish the day you buy it or the next day, otherwise, freeze it. You can also use frozen food and cook it without defrosting.

As little canned and processed food as possible. Canned fruits and vegetables are overcooked. Most canned vegetables contain salt and canned fruit contains sugar. Most canned fish also contains salt. Choose products that don't. Canned legumes are not very salty, but they need to be rinsed. Processed meat (e.g., deli meat) is not suitable for babies.

Organically grown or not. Organic fruits and vegetables contain less pesticide residue than regular products. Non-organic produce still offers more benefits than risks, and it is important that babies eat some at every meal. Carefully wash fresh fruit and vegetables and peel them as needed before cooking.

Fish with fewer contaminants. Avoid fish caught in polluted lakes or from sport fishing, and avoid large predators. (See *Fish*, p. 49.)

Ideally you want to cook food as soon as possible after buying it to maximize its nutritional value. Avoid overcooking fruits and vegetables, and make sure you cook meat, poultry, fish and eggs to prevent food poisoning. Follow rules of hygiene when you prepare your baby's meals (see *Prevent Food Poisoning*, p. 64).

Steamed. Cooking in a steamer basket or saucepan made for steaming. This method of cooking requires very little water, and the food doesn't soak in it. It is quick and retains the nutritional value of food.

Microwave. Very fast cooking and very little, if any, water. It preserves the nutritional value of food. The waves are not a danger for babies' health because they do not remain in the food.

Pressure cooker. Pressure cookers cook food three times faster than a regular saucepan. Food cooks in minimal liquid. Its nutritional value remains high.

In liquid. Cooking in a saucepan, in simmering liquid (water, broth or milk). The cooking liquid and seasonings lend flavor to the food. However, food loses vitamins and minerals as they leach out into the liquid. Use a small amount and reuse the liquid to make vegetable, fruit, meat, poultry and fish purées.

In the oven. In a covered or uncovered dish, en papillote or roasted. This is the ideal method for cooking vegetables such as beets and squash before peeling them and for preparing tender meat stews.

Slow cooker. Slow cooking at a low temperature. This method lets you prepare a wide range of dishes, which cook while you're doing other things; not to be sneezed at! It makes meat, poultry and fish tender. Because the cooking is slow, vegetables lose a significant amount of their vitamins and minerals. So it is not the best method of cooking for vegetables. Add them at the end of cooking to avoid them being overcooked.

Fried food is not recommended for babies.

MAKING PURÉES

To mash or purée food, use the tool you want (e.g., blender, food processor, potato masher, fork). Each one results in a different texture. To get the texture you want, it is easier to purée a little at a time: ½ to 1 cup (125 to 250 ml).

Limit the number of purées you prepare ahead of time, because babies progress quickly in terms of the texture of the food they can eat: around 1 cup (250 ml) of meat or poultry and 2 cups (500 ml) of fruit or vegetables.

For foods that contain a lot of water (e.g., zucchini, cauliflower, pineapple, watermelon), you don't need to add liquid to make a purée. For the rest, add a bit of liquid to give it the consistency you want. Use cooking liquid preferably or add cold water (no need to boil it — see *Water*, p. 56), breast milk, infant formula or broth with no salt. For purées prepared ahead of time, always make them a little thicker: babies will be eating thicker purées in a week or two, plus defrosting thins some purées. It's easier to add liquid than to remove it!

When you're not serving the purée immediately, cool it as quickly as possible in the refrigerator. Refrigerate the purée you plan to use quickly in a tightly closed container. Freeze purée that will be eaten later on. How long it keeps depends on how it is stored: packaging, temperature and how often the fridge or freezer is opened. The freezer compartment of a fridge is not as cold as a chest freezer and is opened more often, which reduces the amount of time you can keep food. (See *How Long to Keep Purées*, p. 76.)

1. Pour the purée into an ice cube tray or silicone muffin tin (mini or regular). Fill some compartments only halfway. (Distribute the purée in small portions so you can defrost only what you need and reduce waste. To start introducing food, use half-portions.)

2. Cover and cool purée in the refrigerator.

3. Put the purée in the freezer for 8 to 12 hours, until frozen.

4. Store cubes or discs of frozen purée in a resealable freezer bag. Remove the air and close tightly. Write the name of the food and the date it was cooked on the bag. Return to the freezer immediately.

HOW LONG TO KEEP PURÉES		
	In the refrigerator (39°F/4°C)	In the freezer (0°F/-18°C)
Vegetables	2 to 3 days	6 to 8 months
Fruits	2 to 3 days	6 to 8 months
Meat, poultry, fish	1 to 2 days	1 to 2 months
Meat, poultry or fish mixed with vegetables	1 to 2 days	1 to 2 months
Legumes, tofu, tempeh	2 to 3 days	2 to 3 months
Pasta, rice, barley, quinoa and other grains	2 to 3 days	2 to 3 months

- If the purée has been frozen, defrost it in the refrigerator 2 to 4 hours in advance and reheat it when you are ready to serve. Fruit, vegetable, legume, tofu and pasta purées must be consumed within two days of defrosting; meat, poultry and fish purées should be consumed within 24 hours.

- Reheat, or rather warm, purée in one of the following ways:
  - In a small saucepan or bain-marie on the stove
  - In a glass bowl placed in a larger bowl of hot water
  - In the microwave

- Be sure to stir the purée well to distribute heat uniformly, particularly if you are using a microwave, because it reheats food unevenly.

- Always check the temperature before serving it to your baby.

- After the meal is done, throw out the remaining reheated purée. **Never put defrosted purée back in the freezer.**

21 DAYS
OF MENUS

The menus in this book were designed to satisfy babies' nutritional and energy needs and to familiarize them with a wide range of foods to develop their tastes.

There are three weeks of menus suitable for different ages: 7 to 8 months, 9 to 11 months and 12 to 18 months. There is no menu before 7 months, because during the first weeks of food diversification, habits and schedules are not sufficiently well established. Even afterwards, the schedule and menus don't change overnight between the 8th and 9th month, for example. They have to be flexible and suited to your baby.

Snacks are suggested in the menu. Integrate them gradually and offer a snack only if your baby is hungry. There is no regular snack planned for the evening, but if your child needs one, offer one. Suggestions for snacks appear at the beginning of each menu section.

Breastfeed when your baby wants to. Breastfeeding times in menus are just suggestions. The term "breast milk" is used to simplify menus. If your baby is not breast fed, give him or her infant formula (or cow's milk beginning at age 9 months, only if your baby has a good appetite for a wide variety of foods). An illustration of a baby bottle is used to indicate feedings (breast milk or infant formula).

There are no suggestions for portions or quantities, because babies are the ones who decide. Their needs are unique. Let them eat until they are full. But you can start off with the portions suggested in the section *Vary Their Diet: Foods To Serve and Avoid*, p. 46, and adjust as you go along.

7 TO 8 MONTHS

From age 7 to 8 months, babies will eat more and more often and in increasing amounts. One month after introducing the first complementary foods, they will eat around three meals and one snack a day. They may be hungry for a snack in the morning and afternoon, or milk may be enough for them. Watch them carefully: they will let you know. We have suggested only an afternoon snack on the menu. Add one in the morning if you need to.

To include in the menu:

- A feeding upon waking, and at least three others during the day, for a minimum of 3 cups (750 ml) in total.
- A feeding before or after solid food depending on how hungry babies are. Food shouldn't limit their appetite for breast milk, because it is the priority at their age. Up to around 7 months, offer them breast milk with solid food at meal times. Beginning at 7 months or when they are hungry enough to eat more, give them breast milk after solid food.
- Two or three meals with food that is high in iron.
- A fruit or vegetable at each meal, or a fruit and a vegetable if babies are hungry enough.
- Different colored foods for a range of nutritional elements.
- At each meal, at least one food they are familiar with and like.
- Regularly, new foods or foods babies didn't like the first time around.
- Portions that reflect their hunger or appetite.

You can choose the fruits and vegetables according to what you are eating. Prepare a portion of vegetables from your menu so they are suitable for your baby (puréed or in soft pieces). A number of recipes in the third section suggest additional ingredients or ways of preparing them for the rest of the family.

At this age, for a snack you can offer them:

- Fruit purée or soft fruit
- Unsweetened oat loops cereal
- Bread crusts
- A piece of toast or pita bread
- Plain 4% to 10% M.F. yogurt

Waking
Breast milk

BREAKFAST

Enriched baby cereal
Apple (Apple Purée, p. 130)
Breast milk

LUNCH

Tofu (Tofu Purée p. 138)
Broccoli (Broccoli Purée, p. 110)
Breast milk

Snack
Unsweetened oat loops cereal

DINNER

Enriched baby cereal
Zucchini (Zucchini Purée, p. 115)
Cantaloupe
Breast milk

Snack
Breast milk

7 to 8 MONTHS
DAY 2

Waking
Breast milk

BREAKFAST

Enriched baby cereal
Peaches (Peach Purée, p. 124)
Breast milk

LUNCH

Romano beans (Romano Bean Purée, p. 118)
Sweet potato (Sweet Potato Purée, p. 123)
Breast milk

Snack
Pineapple (Pineapple Purée, p. 106)

DINNER

Egg
Asparagus (Asparagus Purée, p. 107)
Strawberries (Strawberry Purée, p. 116)
Breast milk

Snack
Breast milk

Waking
Breast milk

BREAKFAST

Enriched baby cereal
Prunes (Prune Purée, p. 136)
Breast milk

LUNCH

Lentils (Lentil Purée, p. 120)
Red pepper (Red Pepper Purée, p. 128)
Breast milk

Snack
Unsweetened oat loops cereal

DINNER

Enriched baby cereal
Butternut squash (Butternut Squash Purée, p. 112)
Pineapple (Pineapple Purée, p. 106)
Breast milk

Snack
Breast milk

7 TO 8 MONTHS
DAY 4

Waking
Breast milk

BREAKFAST ....

Enriched baby cereal
Peaches (Peach Purée, p. 124)
Breast milk

LUNCH ....

Veal (Veal Purée, p. 140)
Parsnips (Parsnip Purée, p. 122)
Breast milk

Snack
Unsweetened oat loops cereal

DINNER ....

Lentils (Lentil Purée, p. 120)
Red pepper (Red Pepper Purée, p. 128)
Banana
Breast milk

Snack
Breast milk

Waking
Breast milk

BREAKFAST

Enriched baby cereal
Apple (Apple Purée, p. 130)
Breast milk

LUNCH

Chicken (Chicken Purée, p. 135)
Asparagus (Asparagus Purée, p. 107)
Breast milk

Snack
Peaches (Peach Purée, p. 124)

DINNER

Tofu (Tofu Purée, p. 138)
Broccoli (Broccoli Purée, p. 110)
Cantaloupe
Breast milk

Snack
Breast milk

Waking
Breast milk

BREAKFAST

Enriched baby cereal
Prunes (Prune Purée, p. 136)
Breast milk

LUNCH

Chicken (Chicken Purée, p. 135)
Beets (Beet Purée, p. 108)
Breast milk

Snack
Strawberries (Strawberry Purée, p. 116)

DINNER

Trout (Trout Purée, p. 139)
Peas (Pea Purée, p. 126)
Apples and pears (Apple and Pear Purée, p. 132)
Breast milk

Snack
Breast milk

Waking
Breast milk

BREAKFAST

Enriched baby cereal
Apples and pears (Apple and Pear Purée, p. 132)
Breast milk

LUNCH

Trout (Trout Purée, p. 139)
Zucchini (Zucchini Purée, p. 115)
Breast milk

Snack
Banana

DINNER

Veal (Veal Purée, p. 140)
Cauliflower (variation of Broccoli Purée, p. 110)
Apples and plums (variation of Apple and Pear Purée, p. 132)
Breast milk

Snack
Breast milk

9 TO 11 MONTHS

From age 9 to 11 months, babies will eat three meals and two or three snacks a day, depending on how hungry they are. Meals will look more and more like your own, made up of foods that are not highly processed. The recipes in this book are suitable for the whole family. Dessert is optional. If you serve it at one or two meals, choose nourishing food, such as the snacks suggested below. And if you are having dessert, offer your baby a serving, no matter how much your baby has eaten as a main course. Don't force your baby to eat, whether vegetables, meat or dessert.

To include in the menu:

- Around 2½ cups to 3 cups (625 to 750 ml) breast milk per day, in as many feedings as your baby wants. Depending on the stage your baby is at, it can be breast milk, infant formula, transition milk or cow's milk.

- Three meals including food that is high in iron.

- At least one fruit or one vegetable at each meal. You can substitute different fruits and vegetables for those suggested on the menus. The important thing is that there is a variety during the day or week. Serve them in a lumpy purée or soft pieces.

- A snack in the morning and the afternoon, light or filling, depending on how hungry your baby is and how long until the next meal. In the sample menus that follow, morning snacks are light (e.g. a piece of fruit), and afternoon snacks are more filling. If your baby is hungry in the evening before going to bed, you can add a snack.

At this age, for a snack you can give them:

- Fruit

- Plain 4% to 10% M.F. yogurt

- Unsweetened oat loops cereal

- Bread crusts

- A piece of toast or pita bread

- A muffin or homemade cookie

- Homemade pudding made with milk, soy beverage or silken tofu

BREAKFAST

Enriched baby cereal
Strawberries (Strawberry Purée, p. 116)
Milk

Snack
Blueberries

LUNCH

Liver Pâté (p. 185)
Egg (poached, hard-boiled or scrambled)
Carrots

Snack
Plain yogurt with compote

DINNER

Mini Lentil Loaves (p. 180)
Barley
Pepper
Clementine

Snack
Breast milk or snack (p. 88) if baby is hungry

9 TO 11 MONTHS
DAY 2

BREAKFAST . . . .

Enriched baby cereal
Banana
Milk

Snack
Strawberries (Strawberry Purée, p. 116)

LUNCH . . . .

Mini Lentil Loaves (p. 180)
Barley
Pepper

Snack
Toast and peanut butter

DINNER . . . .

Maple Chicken Thighs (p. 166)
Potatoes
Green beans
Plain yogurt

Snack
Breast milk or snack (p. 88) if baby is hungry

BREAKFAST

Enriched baby cereal
Mango
Milk

Snack
Banana

LUNCH

Maple Chicken Thighs (p. 166)
Potatoes
Green beans

Snack
Milk and unsweetened oat loops cereal

DINNER

Farfalle with Creamy Pesto Sauce (p. 168)
Butternut squash

Snack
Breast milk or snack (p. 88) if baby is hungry

9 TO 11 MONTHS
DAY 4

BREAKFAST ....

Enriched baby cereal
Pear
Milk

> **Snack**
> Orange

LUNCH ....

Farfalle with Creamy Pesto Sauce (p. 168)
Butternut squash

> **Snack**
> Cheese and kiwi

DINNER ....

Salmon and Tofu Loaf with Cheese Sauce (p. 182)
Asparagus

> **Snack**
> Breast milk or snack (p. 88) if baby is hungry

BREAKFAST ....

Enriched baby cereal
Kiwi
Milk

Snack
Apple (Apple Purée, p. 130)

LUNCH ....

Salmon and Tofu Loaf with Cheese Sauce (p. 182)
Asparagus

Snack
Plain yogurt with compote

DINNER ....

Pasta Frittata (p. 175)
Tomato

Snack
Breast milk or snack (p. 88) if baby is hungry

9 TO 11 MONTHS
DAY 6

BREAKFAST

Enriched baby cereal
Grapes, quartered
Milk

Snack
Pineapple

LUNCH

Macaroni and Cheese (p. 176)
Broccoli
Peanut Butter Pudding (p. 155)

Snack
Strawberry Tofu (p. 160)

DINNER

Meat and Chickpea Balls with Tomato Sauce (p. 162)
Polenta
Brussels sprouts

Snack
Breast milk or snack (p. 88) if baby is hungry

BREAKFAST ....

Enriched baby cereal
Blueberries
Milk

Snack
Orange

LUNCH ....

Meat and Chickpea Balls with Tomato Sauce (p. 162)
Polenta
Brussels sprouts

Snack
Toast and peanut butter

DINNER ....

Nordic Shrimp Risotto (p. 192)
Cucumber

Snack
Breast milk or snack (p. 88) if baby is hungry

12 TO 18 MONTHS

From age 12 to 18 months, babies will have a regular schedule for meals and snacks, and they will share your meals. Serve them three meals and two or three snacks a day depending on their appetite. Choose foods with limited processing. The recipes in this book are suitable for the whole family. Dessert is optional. If you serve it at one or two meals, choose nourishing food, like the snacks suggested below. And if you are having dessert, offer your baby a serving, no matter how much your baby has eaten as a main course. Don't force your baby to eat, whether vegetables, meat or dessert.

To include on the menu:

- 2 cups (500 ml) milk per day, broken down between meals and snacks. Give them a small glass of water in the morning, afternoon and evening.
- Breast milk, depending on your choices and convenience.
- Three meals with foods that are high in iron.
- At least one fruit or one vegetable at each meal. You can substitute different fruits and vegetables for those suggested on the menus. The important thing is that there is a variety during the day or week. Serve them raw or cooked, following the principles to prevent choking (p. 59).
- A snack in the morning and the afternoon, light or filling, depending on how hungry babies are and how long until the next meal. In the sample menus that follow, morning snacks are light (e.g. a piece of fruit), and afternoon snacks are more filling. If babies are hungry in the evening before going to bed, you can add a snack.

At this age, for a snack you can give them:

- Fruit or vegetables with milk or cheese
- Plain 4% to 10% M.F. yogurt with fruit or unsweetened compote
- Unsweetened oat loops cereal with milk or soy beverage
- A muffin or homemade cookie
- Homemade pudding made with milk, soy beverage or silken tofu

12 TO 18 MONTHS

BREAKFAST

Banana Cardamom Mini Muffins (p. 146)
Milk

Snack
Orange and milk

LUNCH

Vegetarian Quinoa (p. 190)
Apple

Snack
Strawberry Tofu (p. 160)

DINNER

Mexican Turnovers (p. 165)
Green salad
Oatmeal Cookies (p. 142)

Snack
Snack (p. 96) if baby is hungry

12 TO 18 MONTHS
DAY 2

BREAKFAST

Toast
Peanut butter
Milk

Snack
Pineapple and milk

LUNCH

Mexican Turnovers (p. 165)
Green salad
Strawberry Tofu (p. 160)

Snack
Peanut butter cookies and milk

DINNER

Mini Indian Meatloaves (p. 186)
Rice
Snow peas
Cantaloupe

Snack
Snack (p. 96) if baby is hungry

BREAKFAST

Prune Mini Muffins (p. 148)
Milk

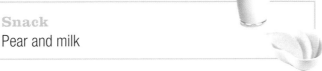

Snack
Pear and milk

LUNCH

Mini Indian Meatloaves (p. 186)
Rice
Snow peas

Snack
Blueberry Scones (p. 156) and yogurt

DINNER

Black Bean Quesadillas (p. 188)
Tomato and cucumber

Snack
Snack (p. 96) if baby is hungry

12 TO 18 MONTHS
DAY 4

BREAKFAST ....

Oatmeal cooked in milk
Milk

Snack
Blueberries and milk

LUNCH ....

Black Bean Quesadillas (p. 188)
Tomato and cucumber

Snack
Banana Pudding (p. 152)

DINNER ....

Spaghetti with Tomato and Red Bean Sauce (p. 196)
Cauliflower
Clementine

Snack
Snack (p. 96) if baby is hungry

BREAKFAST

Liver Pâté (p. 185)
Toast
Milk

Snack
Banana and milk

LUNCH

Spaghetti with Tomato and Red Bean Sauce (p. 196)
Cauliflower
Peach mint yogurt

Snack
Oatmeal Cookies (p. 142) and milk

DINNER

Tofu with Peanut Sauce (p. 198)
Rice
Kiwi

Snack
Snack (p. 96) if baby is hungry

BREAKFAST

Maple Cinnamon Tofu (p. 158)
Toast
Milk

Snack
Cantaloupe and milk

LUNCH

Macaroni and Cheese (p. 176)
Broccoli
Banana Pudding (p. 152)

Snack
Peach mint yogurt

DINNER

Stewed Pork and Vegetables (p. 178)
Potato
Asparagus
Pear

Snack
Snack (p. 96) if baby is hungry

BREAKFAST

Pear Pancakes (p. 150)
Milk

Snack
Plum and milk

LUNCH

Cheese Sandwiches on French Toast (p. 195)
Fruit or vegetable salad

Snack
Pita, cucumber and hummus

DINNER

Crispy Fish Fillets with Almonds (p. 170)
Oven-Baked Sweet Potato Fries (p.172)
Peas
Oatmeal Cookies (p. 142)

Snack
Snack (p. 96) if baby is hungry

RECIPES
50 HEALTHY IDEAS

The recipes in this book will help your child grow up healthy and enjoy a variety of foods. Breakfasts, snacks and main dishes have been created to appeal to the whole family. Some recipes for purées include suggestions for adapting them for adults.

PINEAPPLE
Purée

PREPARATION: 5 minutes

INGREDIENT

½ pineapple, peeled and core removed, in chunks

METHOD

In a mixer or food processor, purée pineapple. Add a bit of water to obtain desired consistency.

TIP

You can use frozen pineapple.

VARIATION

Replace pineapple with mango or pineapple. **Warning**: Wash these fruits before peeling and slicing them to get rid of any dirt or bacteria on the peels. They can come into contact with the flesh of the fruit as you are cutting.

ASPARAGUS
Purée

PREPARATION: 5 minutes • COOKING TIME: 10 minutes

METHOD

Wash asparagus. Remove woody ends and cut stalks into three pieces.

In a steamer, cook asparagus for 10 minutes until tender. (Don't wait until they turn olive green.) Plunge in ice water to stop cooking.

In a blender, purée asparagus. Add a bit of cooking liquid as needed to obtain desired consistency.

. . . .

FOR ADULTS

Cook asparagus in chicken broth with a potato and onion to make soup.

INGREDIENT

1 lb (500 g) asparagus

BEET
Purée

PREPARATION: 5 minutes • COOKING TIME: 45 minutes

INGREDIENT

3 beets

METHOD

Use a vegetable brush to wash beets under cold water. Cut off both ends. Leave whole with peel.

In a saucepan over medium-high heat, cook beets in boiling water for 45 minutes or until tender. Let cool 5 minutes. Peel and slice.

Using a potato masher, blender or fork, purée beets. Add a bit of cooking liquid as needed to obtain desired consistency.

· · · · · · · · · · · · · · ·

FOR ADULTS

Cook extra beets to make soup (beets cooked in chicken broth with a clove of garlic and grated ginger) or a salad (diced beets, grapefruit sections and crumbled goat's cheese).

BABY INFO

It was previously recommended to wait before introducing beets, because of their high natural nitrate content. Now we know that if you introduce them starting at 6 months and serve a variety of vegetables, there is no cause for concern.

BROCCOLI
Purée

STARTING
AT 6 MONTHS

PREPARATION: 5 minutes • COOKING TIME: 10 minutes

INGREDIENT

2 cups (500 ml) broccoli florets

METHOD

In a steamer, cook broccoli for 10 minutes or until tender. (The broccoli should retain its color.)

Using a potato masher or blender, purée broccoli. Add a bit of cooking liquid as needed to obtain desired consistency.

· · · · · · · · · · · · · ·

VARIATION

You can use cauliflower instead of broccoli. Cauliflower needs to cook longer (about 15 minutes).

· · · · · · · · · · · · · ·

FOR ADULTS

- Add 1 tbsp basil pesto to broccoli to make a purée or soup.
- Add ½ cup (125 ml) firm cheese (for instance, Gruyère, old Cheddar, Parmesan) to the cauliflower to make a purée or soup.

BABY INFO

Broccoli can cause gas. It is best to start with a small amount and gradually increase it.

110

BROCCOLI

BUTTERNUT SQUASH
Purée

PREPARATION: 15 minutes • COOKING TIME: 45 minutes

INGREDIENTS

1 butternut squash

1 tbsp olive oil

2 cloves garlic, peeled

METHOD

Place oven rack in center of oven and preheat to 400°F (200°C). Line a baking sheet with parchment paper.

Use a vegetable brush to scrub squash under cold water. Cut in half and scoop out seeds. Brush flesh with oil.

Place squash on prepared baking sheet, skin side up, and place a clove of garlic under each half. Bake in preheated oven for 45 minutes or until flesh is tender. Let cool to room temperature.

Remove flesh from squash using a soupspoon. Using a potato masher, blender or fork, purée squash, one half at a time. (Do not combine two halves.) Add a bit of water as needed to achieve desired consistency.

Add crushed garlic cloves to one of two portions. (Use this one to prepare a purée for adults — see *For Adults* — or freeze it to serve to your baby once your baby is used to the taste of plain squash.

FOR ADULTS

To the purée, add garlic cloves, 1 tbsp brown butter (melted butter heated until it turns brown) and pepper. Serve with grilled meat or stew.

ZUCCHINI
Purée

PREPARATION: 5 minutes • **COOKING TIME:** 5 minutes

METHOD

Use a vegetable brush to scrub zucchini under cold water. Cut in half rounds or large dice.

In a steamer, cook zucchini for 4 or 5 minutes or until very tender.

Using a potato masher or blender, purée zucchini. (There is no point in adding water, because zucchini contains enough already.)

INGREDIENT

2 zucchinis

BABY INFO

Zucchini purée has a very mild flavor that most babies like. But later on, many of them will reject the texture of cooked pieces of zucchini. Getting babies used to the taste of zucchini as long as they like purées increases the chance that they will like it as they are growing up.

STRAWBERRY
Purée

PREPARATION: 5 minutes

INGREDIENT

2 cups (500 ml) ripe strawberries, hulled

METHOD

Wash strawberries under cold water.

Use a fork or blender to purée strawberries. If you want, press through a strainer to remove seeds. Add a bit of water to obtain desired consistency.

. . . .

VARIATION

Use raspberries or blueberries instead of strawberries. They can all be pressed through a strainer to remove seeds, if you want.

. . . .

TIP

You can use frozen fruit. Defrost before puréeing.

BABY INFO

Store-bought strawberry purée is often a strawberry dessert with added sugar. Homemade strawberry purée is better for your baby.

ROMANO BEAN
Purée

PREPARATION: 5 minutes • **SOAKING TIME:** 8 hours • **COOKING TIME:** 1 hour

INGREDIENTS

1 cup (250 ml) Romano beans

4 cups (1 liter) water

METHOD

In a bowl, combine beans and water. Refrigerate for 8 to 12 hours. Discard soaking liquid.

Place beans in a saucepan with cold water. Cover and bring to a boil over medium-high heat, then simmer over low heat for 1 hour or until beans are tender. Drain.

Use a blender or fork to purée 1 cup (250 ml) beans at a time with 3 tbsp water. Add a bit of water as needed obtain desired consistency.

TIPS

- You can use canned beans. Choose low-sodium beans. Rinse and drain beans before puréeing.

- You can also cook beans in a pressure cooker: it is four times faster.

VARIATION

Use red, white, black, pinto or other beans. If you use red beans for this recipe, you can make Tomato and Red Bean Sauce (p. 196) at the same time.

BABY INFO

Like all legumes, Romano beans can cause gas. It is best to start with a small amount (1 to 2 tbsp) and gradually increase.

LENTIL
Purée

PREPARATION: 5 minutes • **SOAKING TIME:** 4 hours • **COOKING TIME:** 10 minutes

INGREDIENTS

1 cup (250 ml) red lentils

4 cups (1 liter) water

METHOD

In a bowl, combine lentils and water. Refrigerate for 6 hours. Discard soaking liquid.

Place lentils in a saucepan with cold water. Cover and bring to a boil over medium-high heat, then simmer over low heat for 10 minutes or until lentils are tender. Drain.

Use a blender or fork to purée 1 cup (250 ml) lentils at a time with 3 tbsp water. Add a bit of water as needed obtain desired consistency.

• • • • • • • • • • • • • •

VARIATION

Use brown or green lentils rather than red lentils.

• • • • • • • • • • • • • •

TIPS

• Unlike beans (red, white, black, Romano, etc.), you can cook lentils without soaking beforehand. But soaking reduces cooking time and makes them easier to digest, so it is good idea to soak lentils when you start introducing them.

• You can also use canned lentils. Choose low-sodium lentils. Rinse and drain them thoroughly before puréeing.

PARSNIP
Purée

PREPARATION: 5 minutes • COOKING TIME: 15 minutes

INGREDIENT

4 parsnips

METHOD

Use a vegetable brush to scrub parsnips under cold water. Peel and slice.

In a steamer, cook parsnips for 15 minutes or until tender.

Use a potato masher or blender to purée parsnips. Add a bit of water as needed obtain desired consistency.

. . . .

FOR ADULTS

Combine parsnip purée with mashed potatoes. And, of course, let your baby try a taste.

SWEET POTATO
Purée

PREPARATION: 5 minutes • COOKING TIME: 20 minutes

METHOD

Use a vegetable brush to scrub sweet potatoes under cold water. Peel and cut in large dice.

In a steamer, cook sweet potatoes for 20 minutes or until tender.

Use a potato masher or blender to purée sweet potatoes. Add some water as needed to obtain desired consistency.

• • • • • • • • • • • • • •

FOR ADULTS

Purée sweet potatoes with a bit of chicken broth, butter and pepper.

INGREDIENT

2 small or 1 medium sweet potatoes

PEACH
Purée

PREPARATION: 5 minutes • COOKING TIME: 15 minutes

INGREDIENTS

8 peaches

¼ cup (60 ml) water

METHOD

Wash peaches under cold water. Peel and pit. Cut flesh in pieces.

Place peaches and water in a saucepan. Bring water to a boil over medium-high heat, then simmer over low heat for 15 minutes or until tender.

Use a potato masher, blender or fork to purée peaches with cooking liquid until desired consistency is obtained.

• • • • • • • • • • • • • •

TIP

In season, when peaches are ripe and juicy, there is no need to cook them. Simply peel and core, and they are easy to purée.

BABY INFO

A ripe peach without its peel can be offered as is to babies beginning at age 6 months. They can bite right into it (toothlessly) or just rub it on their chin!

PEA
Purée

PREPARATION: 5 minutes • COOKING TIME: 10 minutes

INGREDIENT

2 cups (500 ml) frozen peas

METHOD

In a steamer, cook peas for 10 minutes or until tender.

Use a potato masher or blender to purée peas. Add a bit of cooking liquid as needed to obtain desired consistency.

. . . .

TIP

Frozen peas are better than canned. They generally have a better color and do not contain added salt.

. . . .

FOR ADULTS

Add a slice of crispy, crumbled pancetta or bacon to pea purée to make a side dish.

BABY INFO

You can serve babies cooked peas as is. They can pick them up by themselves. Trying to grasp the peas with their fingers helps them develop fine motor skills.

RED PEPPER
Purée

STARTING AT 6 MONTHS

PREPARATION: 10 minutes • COOKING TIME: 5 minutes

INGREDIENT

3 red peppers

FOR ADULTS

- Keep roasted peppers without puréeing. Use them on sandwiches or pizza.
- Double the recipe and keep six halves to make a sauce: In a nonstick skillet over medium-high heat, sauté roasted peppers with a clove of crushed garlic. Add ¼ cup (60 ml) white wine and a sprig of fresh rosemary. Reduce. Add ¼ cup (60 ml) chicken broth and simmer over medium-low heat for 5 minutes. In a blender, reduce the mixture to a smooth purée. Use the sauce with chicken breasts or grilled fish. It can also replace the tomato sauce on Mini Lentil Loaves (p. 180).

METHOD

Place rack in top third of oven before pre-heating grill. Line a baking sheet with lightly oiled aluminum foil.

Use a vegetable brush to scrub peppers under cold water. Cut in half and seed. On prepared baking sheet, place peppers, skin side up.

Cook under grill for 5 minutes or until skin is blackened. Remove from oven, wrap in aluminum foil and let cool to room temperature for 5 minutes. (Peppers will release steam, and skin will be easy to remove from flesh.)

Peel peppers.

Use a blender to purée peppers. (There is no point adding water, because peppers contain enough.)

VARIATIONS

- Use the same technique to prepare orange or yellow pepper purée.
- You can roast peppers on the barbecue, skin side down. Place them in a sealed container for 5 to 6 minutes to remove skin easily.

APPLE
Purée

PREPARATION: 5 minutes • COOKING TIME: 15 minutes

INGREDIENTS

8 apples

¼ cup (60 ml) water

METHOD

Use a vegetable brush to scrub apples under cold water. Do not peel. Cut in pieces after coring.

Place apples and water in a saucepan. Bring to a boil over medium-high heat, then simmer over low heat for 15 minutes or until apples are tender.

Use a potato masher or blender to reduce apples to a smooth purée with cooking liquid.

VARIATION

Once babies are familiar with the taste of plain apples, you can add a pinch or stick of cinnamon while cooking (remove the stick before puréeing).

TIP

Many varieties of apples (for instance, McIntosh, Cortland, Vista Bell and Melba) make great applesauce. For babies, if you are keeping the peels, it is better to use organic apples.

BABY INFO

If you buy store-bought applesauce occasionally, choose the kind with no sugar added.

APPLE
and Pear Purée

PREPARATION: 5 minutes • COOKING TIME: 15 minutes

INGREDIENTS

4 apples

4 pears

¼ cup (60 ml) water

METHOD

Use a vegetable brush to scrub apples and pears under cold water. Peel pears. Cut fruit in pieces after coring.

Place apples, pears and water in a saucepan. Bring to a boil over medium-high heat, then simmer over low heat for 15 minutes or until fruit is tender.

Use a potato masher or blender to reduce apples and pears to a smooth purée with cooking liquid.

. . . .

VARIATION

Apples go well with a variety of fruit (for instance, cranberries, strawberries, peaches and plums). You can combine them with apple once babies have tried them separately (except for cranberries, which are not served on their own because they are too bitter).

. . . .

TIPS

- Many varieties of apples (for instance, McIntosh, Cortland, Vista Bell and Melba) make great applesauce. For babies, if you are keeping the peels, it is better to use organic apples.

- If your baby is ready to eat less smooth purées, peel the apples too. This way you can mash the fruit with just a fork.

CHICKEN
Purée

PREPARATION: 15 minutes • COOKING TIME: 30 minutes

METHOD

Place all ingredients in a saucepan and cover. Bring to a boil over medium-high heat, then simmer over low heat for 30 minutes or until chicken is cooked. Remove chicken thighs and let cool on a plate for 10 minutes before deboning.

In a blender, reduce about 1 cup (250 ml) of chicken and ⅓ cup (80 ml) cooking liquid. Add a bit of water as needed to obtain desired consistency. (It is easier to obtain a smooth purée with a small amount of chicken than with a large amount.) Repeat this step once or twice with remaining chicken.

INGREDIENTS

2 skinless chicken thighs
(about 1 lb/500 g)

2 carrots, peeled and cut in sections

2 celery stalks, cut in sections

½ onion, quartered

3 cups (750 ml) water

VARIATION

Use chicken breasts instead of thighs, or use turkey to make turkey purée using this recipe.

TIP

Use the vegetables and the cooking liquid to make soup.

BABY INFO

Leg meat (dark meat) is higher in iron than breast (white meat). And since it contains more fat, it is also more tender.

PRUNE
Purée

PREPARATION: 5 minutes • SOAKING TIME: 10 minutes

INGREDIENTS

1 cup (250 ml) prunes, pitted

1 cup (250 ml) water

METHOD

In a bowl, let prunes soak in water for 10 minutes.

In a blender, purée prunes with water until desired consistency is achieved.

BABY INFO

If your baby tends to be constipated, prune purée can help. In addition to being high in fiber, prunes have a substance that stimulates contractions of the intestine.

TOFU
Purée

PREPARATION: 5 minutes

INGREDIENTS

2 oz (60 g) firm tofu, cut in pieces

2 tbsp breast milk, milk or infant formula

METHOD

In a blender, purée ingredients. Add a bit of milk as needed to obtain desired consistency.

Heat slightly before serving.

. . . .

TIP

You can't freeze this purée. Make a little at a time, for one or two meals to be eaten within three days.

TROUT
Purée

PREPARATION: 10 minutes • COOKING TIME: 5 minutes

METHOD

In a saucepan over low heat, heat milk and poach trout for 5 minutes or until it flakes easily with a fork.

Using a fork or a blender, purée trout with a bit of milk from cooking as needed to obtain desired consistency.

INGREDIENTS

¼ cup (60 ml) whole milk or infant formula

½ lb (250 g) skinless boneless trout fillets

TIP

Run your fingers along raw fish to feel if there are any bones.

VARIATION

Use another fish instead of trout (see *Fish*, p. 49).

VEAL
Purée

PREPARATION: 15 minutes • COOKING TIME: 2 hours

INGREDIENTS

1 lb (500 g) veal cubes

2 carrots, peeled and cut in sections

2 celery stalks, cut in sections

½ onion, quartered

3 cups (750 ml) water

METHOD

Place ingredients in a saucepan and cover. Simmer over low heat for 2 hours or until meat can be cut with a fork. Stir every 30 minutes. Let cool, uncovered, for 10 minutes. Separate meat from vegetables. (The vegetables are there to flavor the veal. You can use them in a soup.)

In a blender, purée about 1 cup (250 ml) veal and ⅓ cup (80 ml) cooking liquid. Add a bit of cooking liquid as needed to obtain desired consistency. (It is easier to obtain a smooth purée with a small amount of veal than with a large amount.) Repeat this step once or twice with remaining veal.

VARIATION

Use beef, pork, emu or ostrich cubes instead of veal.

TIPS

• You can cook the meat in a pressure cooker for around 30 minutes.

• You can use very tender meat from a stew (p. 178) or one of your pressure cooker recipes and purée a portion for your baby. But don't add salt to the stew. Wait until you have removed your baby's portion before adding any.

OATMEAL
Cookies

36 cookies • **PREPARATION:** 10 minutes • **COOKING TIME:** 10 minutes

INGREDIENTS

1 cup (250 ml) enriched baby cereal

½ cup (125 ml) quick-cooking oats

½ cup (125 ml) all-purpose flour

1 tsp baking soda

½ tsp ground nutmeg

⅓ cup (80 ml) unsalted butter

¼ cup (60 ml) brown sugar

⅓ cup (80 ml) unsweetened applesauce

2 eggs

1 tsp vanilla extract

METHOD

Place rack in top third of oven and preheat to 375°F (190°C). Line two baking sheets with parchment paper.

In a bowl, combine cereal, oats, flour, baking soda and nutmeg.

In another bowl, using an electric mixer, blend butter and brown sugar until creamy. While mixing, add applesauce, then eggs, one at a time, and vanilla. Pour mixture over dry ingredients and combine gently.

On prepared baking sheets, place about 1 tbsp dough per cookie, leaving about ¾ inch (2 cm) between them.

Bake in preheated oven for 10 minutes or until cookies are lightly golden. Let cool on a rack.

•••••••••••••••

VARIATION

Add ¼ cup (60 ml) ground almonds or hazelnuts to change the flavor and add protein and good fat.

PEANUT BUTTER
Cookies

24 cookies • PREPARATION: 15 minutes • COOKING TIME: 10 minutes

METHOD

Place rack in top third of oven and preheat to 375°F (190°C). Line two baking sheets with parchment paper.

In a bowl, combine flour, cereal and baking powder.

In another bowl, using an electric mixer, blend butter, peanut butter and sugar until creamy. While whisking, add applesauce and egg until mixture is smooth. Using a spoon, add flour and cereal mixture.

On prepared baking sheets, place about 1 tbsp dough per cookie, leaving about ¾ inch (2 cm) between them. Press down lightly with a fork.

Bake in preheated oven for 10 minutes or until cookies are golden. Let cool on a rack.

INGREDIENTS

½ cup (125 ml) whole wheat flour

½ cup (125 ml) enriched baby cereal

1 tsp baking powder

¼ cup (60 ml) softened butter

½ cup (125 ml) natural creamy peanut butter

2 tbsp sugar

⅓ cup (80 ml) unsweetened applesauce

1 egg

BABY INFO

It is a good idea to get babies used to natural peanut butter (made only with peanuts, with no added sugar, salt, oil or additives).

BANANA CARDAMOM
Mini Muffins

20 mini muffins • PREPARATION: 10 minutes • COOKING TIME: 20 minutes

INGREDIENTS

½ cup (125 ml) plain Greek yogurt or plain yogurt

½ tsp baking soda

½ cup (125 ml) all-purpose flour

½ cup (125 ml) cream of wheat

1 tsp baking powder

¼ tsp ground cardamom

¼ tsp salt

½ cup (125 ml) canola oil

1 tbsp brown sugar

1 egg

1 banana, mashed

METHOD

Place rack in center of oven and preheat to 350°F (180°C).

In a bowl, combine yogurt and baking soda. (Use at least a 2-cup/500 ml bowl because yogurt will expand.) Let sit for 5 minutes.

Meanwhile, in another bowl, combine flour, cream of wheat, baking powder, cardamom and salt.

In another bowl, using a whisk, combine oil and brown sugar. Add egg while whisking, then banana and yogurt. Combine thoroughly. Add dry ingredients and gently combine with a spoon.

Distribute batter in a nonstick or silicone mini-muffin tin, filling to ⅔. Bake in preheated oven for 20 minutes or until a toothpick inserted in center comes out clean. Let cool to room temperature before turning out.

• • • • • • • • • • • • • • •

VARIATIONS

- If you don't have a mini-muffin tin, use regular size. Extend baking time by about 10 minutes.

- You can use ground cinnamon or nutmeg instead of cardamom.

PRUNE
Mini Muffins

STARTING AT 9 MONTHS

36 mini muffins • **PREPARATION:** 20 minutes • **COOKING TIME:** 15 minutes

INGREDIENTS

1 cup (250 ml) all-purpose flour

1 cup (250 ml) enriched baby cereal

1 tsp baking powder

½ tsp baking soda

¼ tsp salt

½ cup (125 ml) canola oil

¼ cup (60 ml) sugar

2 eggs

1 cup (250 ml) Prune Purée
(see recipe p. 136)

½ cup (125 ml) plain Greek yogurt or
plain yogurt

Zest of 1 well-scrubbed orange

1 tsp vanilla extract

METHOD

Place rack in center of oven and preheat to 350°F (180°C).

In a bowl, combine flour, cereal, baking powder, baking soda and salt.

In another bowl, using a whisk, combine oil and sugar. Add eggs, one at a time, whisking after each addition. Add prune purée, yogurt, orange zest and vanilla. Combine. Add dry ingredients and gently combine.

Distribute batter in a nonstick or silicone mini-muffin tin, filling to ⅔. Bake in preheated oven for 15 minutes or until a toothpick inserted in center comes out clean. Let cool to room temperature before turning out.

• • • • • • • • • • • • • •

VARIATION

If you don't have a mini-muffin tin, use regular size. Extend baking time by about 10 minutes.

PEAR
Pancakes

5 pancakes • PREPARATION: 15 minutes • COOKING TIME: 30 minutes

INGREDIENTS

1 egg

1 cup (250 ml) milk

1 tsp vanilla extract

1 pear, washed and grated

½ cup (125 ml) whole wheat flour

¼ cup (60 ml) cream of wheat

METHOD

In a bowl, using a whisk, combine egg and milk. Add vanilla and pear.

In another bowl, combine flour and cream of wheat. Using a spoon, incorporate with the moist ingredients. Gently combine.

In a small nonstick skillet over medium-low heat, pour about ⅓ cup (80 ml) batter. Cook for 3 minutes or until underside of pancake is golden. Turn and continue cooking a few minutes to brown other side. Repeat with remaining batter.

Serve pancakes on their own or with plain yogurt, fruit compote or a thin layer of almond butter.

BABY INFO

Like enriched baby cereal, cream of wheat is high in iron.

BANANA
Pudding

4 portions • PREPARATION: 5 minutes • REFRIGERATION TIME: 2 hours

INGREDIENTS

½ cup (125 ml) plain soy beverage

1 very ripe banana

½ cup (125 ml) plain yogurt or plain Greek yogurt

½ tsp vanilla extract

2 tbsp chia seeds

1 star anise

METHOD

In a blender or stand mixer, combine soy beverage and banana until smooth.

Transfer mixture to a bowl and stir in yogurt, vanilla, chia seeds and anise.

Pour into a sealable container and refrigerate for 2 hours. Remove star anise before serving.

• • • • • • • • • • • • • •

VARIATION

You can replace soy beverage with coconut or almond beverage. But soy beverage is the most nourishing choice.

BABY INFO

Babies are happy with the naturally sweet taste of food. It is important to instill good habits in them.

PEANUT BUTTER
Pudding

4 portions • PREPARATION: 10 minutes • COOKING TIME: 5 minutes

METHOD

In a small saucepan, whisk all ingredients together. Heat over medium-low heat, stirring constantly, for 6 minutes or until thickened.

Pour into a sealable container. Place plastic wrap directly on pudding to prevent skin from forming.

Serve warm or chilled.

INGREDIENTS

1 cup (250 ml) soy beverage

⅓ cup (80 ml) natural creamy peanut butter

1 tbsp maple syrup

2 tbsp cornstarch

BABY INFO

Avoiding peanuts does not prevent allergies. On the contrary, by serving babies peanuts at an early age you can better prevent a peanut allergy.

BLUEBERRY
Scones

8 servings • PREPARATION: 20 minutes • COOKING TIME: 20 minutes

INGREDIENTS

½ cup (125 ml) all-purpose flour

1 cup (250 ml) enriched baby cereal

1 tsp baking powder

1 tbsp sugar

½ tsp salt

Zest of 1 well-scrubbed lemon

3 tbsp cold unsalted butter, diced

½ cup (125 ml) milk

½ cup (125 ml) fresh blueberries (see Tip)

METHOD

Place rack in upper third of oven and preheat to 375°F (190°C). Line a baking sheet with parchment paper.

In food processor, combine flour, cereal, baking powder, sugar, salt and lemon zest. Add butter, pulsing a number of times for a few seconds until consistency is granular. Add milk and combine gently.

Place half of the dough on prepared baking sheet. With your hands or a rolling pin, shape a disc about ¾ inch (2 cm) thick. Spread blueberries on top of dough.

On work surface, with remaining dough, form a second disc the same diameter as first. Place on top of blueberries. Press down using hands or rolling pin. Cut into 8 points, and space them out slightly.

Bake in preheated oven for 20 minutes or until scones are golden. Let cool on baking sheet.

VARIATION

Use different fruit (e.g. raspberries, strawberries, diced peaches) and use zest from the citrus fruit of your choice. You can also just make lemon scones and add fruit.

TIP

Ideally, use fresh blueberries, because frozen blueberries will color the dough. The scones will still be delicious.

MAPLE CINNAMON
Tofu

1 serving • PREPARATION: 10 minutes • COOKING TIME: 10 minutes

INGREDIENTS

2 oz (60 g) firm tofu, diced

2 tsp maple syrup

2 tbsp water

1 tbsp cornstarch

½ tsp ground cinnamon

1 tbsp canola or peanut oil

METHOD

Use paper towel to press tofu to remove excess water.

In a small bowl, combine maple syrup and water. Set aside.

In another bowl, combine cornstarch and cinnamon. Then add tofu and coat it well.

In a skillet, heat oil over medium-high heat. Add tofu and brown for 8 minutes, stirring occasionally to brown all sides.

Pour in maple syrup and reduce for about 2 minutes. Let cool before serving.

Serve with a slice of toast and fruit.

BABY INFO

Babies enjoy the flavor and texture of tofu and, more importantly, they don't have any prejudice against it. To make it naturally part of their lives, it is a good idea to include it regularly on the menu from a young age.

STRAWBERRY
Tofu

4 servings • PREPARATION: 15 minutes • REFRIGERATION TIME: 2 hours

INGREDIENTS

3 cups (750 ml) frozen strawberries

10 oz (300 g) silken tofu

10 fresh basil leaves, chopped (optional)

2 tbsp cornstarch

2 tbsp maple syrup

METHOD

In a saucepan over medium-low heat, cook strawberries for 5 minutes or until tender. Using an immersion blender, purée strawberries, then add tofu and basil. Purée again.

In a small bowl, dilute cornstarch in maple syrup. Pour into saucepan and simmer over low heat, stirring constantly, for about 5 minutes or until thickened.

Distribute mixture into dessert bowls or one large bowl. Place plastic wrap directly on mixture to prevent a skin from forming. Refrigerate for at least 2 hours before serving.

BABY INFO

You can get store-bought flavored and sweetened tofu, but it is better to use the plain version.

MEAT AND CHICKPEA BALLS
with Tomato Sauce

STARTING AT 9 MONTHS

40 meatballs • PREPARATION: 30 minutes • COOKING TIME: 30 minutes

INGREDIENTS

For the meatballs

1 cup (250 ml) cooked chickpeas
or ½ can (19 oz/540 ml) chickpeas,
drained and rinsed

¼ cup (60 ml) milk

1 lb (500 g) ground veal or pork

¼ cup (60 ml) breadcrumbs

1 egg, lightly beaten

¼ cup (60 ml) grated Parmesan

2 cloves garlic, crushed

½ cup (125 ml) fresh parsley, chopped

¼ tsp ground nutmeg

1 tbsp olive oil

Pepper

For the sauce

1 tbsp olive oil

1 shallot, chopped

1 clove garlic, crushed

1 can (28 oz/796 ml) crushed tomatoes

1 cup (250 ml) water

METHOD

In a food processor or stand mixer, purée chickpeas with milk. Place in a bowl and add remaining meatball ingredients, except oil. Use your hands to shape into about 40 meatballs, about 1 inch (2.5 cm) in diameter. Set aside.

In a saucepan over medium-high heat, heat 1 tbsp olive oil and brown shallot for 2 minutes. Add garlic and continue cooking for 1 minute. Add tomatoes and water. Cover and simmer over low heat for 15 minutes.

Meanwhile, in a large skillet or wok with a cover over medium-high heat, heat 1 tbsp oil and uniformly brown meatballs for about 15 minutes.

Add sauce, cover and simmer over low heat for at least 15 minutes. Season with pepper to taste.

Serve with a green vegetable and polenta or pasta.

MEXICAN
Turnovers

4 servings • PREPARATION: 20 minutes • COOKING TIME: 15 minutes

METHOD

Place rack in center of oven and preheat to 350°F (180°C). Line a baking sheet with parchment paper.

In a large skillet or wok, heat oil over medium-high heat. Add onion and brown for 2 minutes. Add garlic and cumin, stirring, for 30 seconds. Add chicken, tomato paste and yogurt and stir for 5 minutes or until mixture is hot. Add Cheddar cheese, then add cilantro. Season with pepper.

On work surface, spread mixture in center of tortillas. Close each tortilla by first folding opposite sides then rolling in other direction to create a turnover.

Place turnovers on prepared baking sheet and bake in preheated oven for 15 minutes.

Serve turnovers with a chopped green salad.

• • • • • • • • • • • • • •

FOR ADULTS

Add ½ tsp hot pepper paste to mixture after taking out your baby's portion.

INGREDIENTS

1 tbsp olive oil

½ onion, finely chopped

2 cloves garlic, crushed

1 tbsp ground cumin

3 cups (750 ml) cooked chicken

½ can (5½ oz/156 ml) tomato paste

⅓ cup (80 ml) plain yogurt or plain Greek yogurt

1 cup (250 ml) grated old Cheddar cheese

⅓ cup (80 ml) chopped fresh cilantro

8 whole wheat tortillas, each about 6 inches (15 cm)

Pepper

MAPLE CHICKEN
Thighs

4 servings • **PREPARATION:** 10 minutes • **REFRIGERATION TIME:** 4 hours • **COOKING TIME:** 50 minutes

INGREDIENTS

4 whole chicken legs (about 2 lbs/1 kg)

For the marinade

¼ cup (60 ml) canola oil

1 tbsp balsamic vinegar

1 tbsp Dijon mustard

2 tbsp maple syrup

1 clove garlic, crushed

METHOD

Place marinade ingredients in a resealable freezer bag. Close and shake. Add chicken legs and coat in marinade. Marinate in sealed bag in refrigerator for at least 4 hours.

Place rack in center of oven and preheat to 400°F (200°C). Line a baking sheet with parchment paper.

Place chicken legs on prepared baking sheet and bake in preheated oven for 50 minutes or until juices run clear when chicken is pierced and meat detaches easily from the bone.

Serve with mashed potatoes and a green vegetable.

BABY INFO

Remove the skin from chicken before serving it to your baby. The skin will keep the meat tender while cooking, but it is nothing but fat. Plus it is hard to chew.

FARFALLE
with Creamy Pesto Sauce

3 servings • PREPARATION: 20 minutes • COOKING TIME: 15 minutes

INGREDIENTS

2 tbsp flaked almonds

8 oz (225 g) farfalle or other short pasta

1 cup (250 ml) packed fresh basil

½ clove garlic, crushed

½ cup (125 ml) grated Parmesan

2 tbsp olive oil

1 cup (250 ml) cooked white beans or ⅔ can (19 oz/540 ml) white beans, drained and rinsed

¼ cup (60 ml) 15% M.F. cream

Pepper

METHOD

In a skillet over medium heat, brown almonds. Let cool.

Meanwhile, in a saucepan over high heat, bring water to a boil. Add pasta and stir to prevent it sticking to the bottom. Follow package instructions to cook.

Drain, reserving ½ cup (125 ml) cooking liquid.

In a food processor, chop basil, garlic, Parmesan and almonds. Add oil in a thin stream, then beans and cream. Process until smooth. Add 4 tbsp reserved cooking liquid and season with pepper to taste.

In a bowl, combine pasta and pesto. Add cooking liquid as needed to obtain desired consistency.

Serve with slices of grilled butternut squash, steamed carrots or thin strips of raw pepper.

CRISPY FISH FILLETS
with Almonds

STARTING AT 9 MONTHS

4 servings • **PREPARATION:** 15 minutes • **COOKING TIME:** 15 minutes

INGREDIENTS

4 to 6 sole, tilapia or halibut fillets (about 14 oz/390 g)

⅓ cup (80 ml) all-purpose flour

2 eggs

¾ cup (180 ml) almonds, ground

¼ cup (60 ml) cornmeal

1 tsp dried oregano

Zest of 2 well-scrubbed lemons

2 tbsp olive oil or butter, divided

Salt and pepper

METHOD

Pat fish fillets with paper towel or clean dishtowel. Set aside.

Place flour in a deep dish.

In a second deep dish, beat eggs.

In a third deep dish, combine almonds, cornmeal, oregano and lemon zest. Season with salt and pepper.

Dredge fillets one by one in flour and shake off excess. Dip in eggs, then coat in almond mixture. Set aside on a large plate.

In a nonstick skillet over medium-high heat, heat 1 tbsp of the oil and cook half of the fish fillets for 3 minutes or until golden on top. Turn and continue cooking for 3 minutes or until flesh is opaque. Repeat with remaining fillets and oil. (You can cook all fillets at same time if skillet is large enough.)

Serve with oven-baked sweet potato fries (p. 172) and a green vegetable.

BABY INFO

Almond coating increases the amount of fiber, good fat and vitamins in a meal, more than breadcrumbs, which are often used for breading food.

OVEN-BAKED
Sweet Potato Fries

4 servings • **PREPARATION:** 10 minutes • **COOKING TIME:** 30 minutes

INGREDIENTS

3 sweet potatoes

3 tbsp cornstarch

1 tsp garlic powder

1 tsp dried rosemary

½ tsp pepper

METHOD

Place rack in center of oven and preheat oven to 425°F (220°C). Grease or line a baking sheet with parchment paper.

Using a vegetable brush, scrub sweet potatoes under cold water. Cut into fries.

In a large bowl, combine cornstarch, garlic powder, rosemary and pepper. Add sweet potatoes and coat well.

Place sweet potato fries on prepared baking sheet. Bake in preheated oven for 30 minutes, turning fries midway through cooking.

Serve with fish or meat.

BABY INFO

Babies love sweet potato purée. To make sure they keep enjoying sweet potatoes, serve them in different forms as they grow.

PASTA
Frittata

4 servings • PREPARATION: 10 minutes • COOKING TIME: 20 minutes

METHOD

In a large bowl, whisk together eggs and milk. Add remaining ingredients except oil then combine with a spoon.

In a large ovenproof skillet, heat oil over low heat. Add egg mixture and cook for 12 minutes or until top is no longer runny.

Place rack in upper third of oven and pre-heat grill.

If handle of skillet is plastic, wrap it in aluminum foil. Grill in oven for 4 minutes or until top of frittata is golden.

Serve with vegetables.

• • • • • • • • • • • • • • •

VARIATION

Use any pasta leftovers: with meat, tomato or rosée sauce or with pesto, seafood, lemon, etc.

INGREDIENTS

3 eggs

¼ cup (60 ml) milk

2 cups (500 ml) leftover pasta in sauce

1 cup (250 ml) grated mozzarella cheese

¼ cup (60 ml) grated Parmesan cheese

¼ cup (60 ml) fresh parsley, chopped

1 tbsp olive oil

MACARONI
and Cheese

3 servings • **PREPARATION:** 10 minutes • **COOKING TIME:** 15 minutes

INGREDIENTS

8 oz (225 g) macaroni or other short pasta

2 tbsp butter

2 tbsp all-purpose flour

½ tsp garlic powder

¾ cup (180 ml) low-sodium chicken broth

¾ cup (180 ml) milk

1 cup (250 ml) grated old Cheddar or mozzarella cheese

½ cup (125 ml) grated Parmesan

Pepper

METHOD

In a saucepan over high heat, bring water to a boil. Add pasta and stir to prevent it sticking to the bottom. Follow instructions on package for al dente cooking.

Meanwhile, in a saucepan over medium heat, melt butter. Add flour and stir for 1 minute. Add garlic powder, broth and milk and stir until mixture thickens.

Add cheese and stir until melted. Season with pepper to taste, then add pasta.

Serve with a green vegetable.

BABY INFO

At least half your pasta meals should be made with whole wheat pasta.

STEWED PORK
and Vegetables

4 servings • **PREPARATION:** 20 minutes • **COOKING TIME:** 4 hours

INGREDIENTS

2 tbsp olive oil (approx.)

1 lb (500 g) pork stewing cubes

1 onion, coarsely chopped

3 cloves garlic, chopped

½ rutabaga, peeled and cut in large cubes

3 carrots, peeled and cut in sections

3 stalks celery, cut in sections

1 cup (250 ml) apple juice

2 cups (500 ml) homemade or low-sodium chicken broth

1 tbsp old-fashioned mustard

¼ cup (60 ml) 15% M.F. cream

METHOD

Place rack in lower third of oven and preheat to 275°F (140°C).

In a large ovenproof saucepan or casserole, heat oil over medium-high heat. Add meat and brown. Set aside on a plate.

In same saucepan, brown onion for 3 minutes or until lightly golden. Add more oil as needed. Add garlic, rutabaga, carrots and celery. Cook, stirring, for 2 to 3 minutes.

Add meat, apple juice, broth and mustard. Cover and bake in preheated oven for 4 hours or until meat comes apart with a fork. Pour a bit of water over stew every hour while cooking.

Remove from oven, add cream and stir gently.

Serve with mashed potatoes and a brightly colored vegetable.

• • • • • • • • • • • • • •

VARIATION

You can add potatoes to the pot for an all-in-one dish. Add them around 1 hour before the stew is done.

MINI LENTIL
Loaves

8 mini loaves • PREPARATION: 15 minutes • COOKING TIME: 30 minutes

INGREDIENTS

2 cups (500 ml) cooked lentils or
1 can (19 oz/540 ml) lentils, drained
and rinsed

1 green onion, chopped

1 cup (250 ml) grated mozzarella

¼ cup (60 ml) breadcrumbs

1 egg, lightly beaten

½ tsp dried oregano

1 tsp dried basil

For the tomato sauce

1 can (5½ oz/156 ml) tomato paste

¼ cup (60 ml) water

1 tsp ground cumin

½ tsp garlic powder

METHOD

Place rack in center of oven and preheat to 350°F (180°C).

In a bowl, using a spoon, combine lentils, green onion, cheese, breadcrumbs, egg, oregano and basil. Spread mixture in a nonstick or silicone muffin tin. Press down lightly.

In a bowl, combine tomato paste, water, cumin and garlic powder. Place 2 tbsp of sauce on each mini lentil loaf.

Bake in preheated oven for 30 minutes.

Serve with a brightly colored vegetable and barley or rice.

. . . .

VARIATIONS

- Use any lentils you like: brown, green or red.

- You can use a store-bought tomato or pasta sauce of your choice rather than homemade or serve with Red Pepper Purée (p. 128).

SALMON AND TOFU LOAF
with Cheese Sauce

3 servings • PREPARATION: 25 minutes • COOKING TIME: 45 minutes

INGREDIENTS

For the loaf

1 can (14.75 oz/418 g) Pacific salmon, flaked with a fork

5 oz (150 g) firm tofu, grated

2 eggs, lightly beaten

¼ cup (60 ml) breadcrumbs

3 green onions, chopped

2 tbsp grated ginger

3 tbsp lemon juice

Pepper

For the sauce

2 tbsp butter

2 tbsp all-purpose flour

1 tsp smoked paprika

½ tsp onion powder

1½ cups (375 ml) milk

1 cup (250 ml) grated old Cheddar cheese

Pepper

METHOD

Place rack in center of oven and preheat to 350°F (180°C).

Line bottom and two long sides of a 9 x 6 inch (23 x 15 cm) bread tin with parchment paper. Butter both sides.

In a bowl, using a spoon, combine all ingredients for loaf. If needed, use hands to mix until well combined.

Pour mixture in prepared bread tin and press with back of spoon or hands. Bake in preheated oven for 45 minutes.

Meanwhile, in a saucepan over medium heat, melt butter. Add flour, paprika and onion powder. Stir for 1 minute. Add milk and stir until mixture thickens. Add cheese and stir until completely melted. Season with pepper to taste.

When ready to serve, turn loaf out and slice. Spoon cheese sauce on top.

Serve with a green vegetable.

LIVER
Pâté

Around ½ lb (250 g) • **PREPARATION:** 10 minutes • **COOKING TIME:** 20 minutes • **REFRIGERATION:** 4 hours

METHOD

In a saucepan, heat oil over medium-high heat. Add shallot and brown for 2 minutes. Add garlic and cook for 1 minute. Add broth and chicken thigh. Cover and simmer over low heat for 15 minutes.

Add liver and simmer for another 5 minutes or until meat is cooked. Remove chicken bone.

In a food processor or using an immersion blender, purée mixture until smooth, adding butter. Add a bit of broth or cream, depending on consistency desired. Season with pepper to taste.

Pour mixture into ramekins and refrigerate for at least 4 hours.

Serve with homemade croutons, low-sodium crackers or toast.

INGREDIENTS

1 tbsp canola oil
1 small shallot, chopped
1 clove garlic, chopped
½ cup (125 ml) low-sodium chicken broth
1 whole skinless chicken leg (about ½ lb/250 g)
3½ oz (100 g) veal liver
1 tbsp butter
Pepper
Cream (optional)

BABY INFO

Liver is the meat that is highest in iron. Mixing it with another meat mellows its distinctive taste, which not everyone likes.

MINI INDIAN
Meatloaves

4 servings • **PREPARATION:** 15 minutes • **COOKING TIME:** 40 minutes

INGREDIENTS

For the mini meatloaves

¼ cup (60 ml) quick-cooking oats

2 tbsp milk

1 lb (500 g) ground meat (beef or other red meat)

½ onion, chopped

1 egg, lightly beaten

1 tbsp ground cumin

1 tbsp ground coriander

1 tbsp olive oil

For the yogurt sauce

1 cup (250 ml) plain yogurt or plain Greek yogurt

Zest of 1 well-scrubbed lemon

1 tbsp lemon juice

2 tbsp chopped fresh cilantro

Pepper

METHOD

Place rack in center of oven and preheat to 350°F (180°C). Line a baking sheet with parchment paper.

In a bowl, combine oats and milk. Let sit for 5 minutes.

In another bowl, stirring with a spoon or mixing with your hands, combine ground meat, onion, egg and spices. Add oat mixture. Shape into 3 small rectangular loaves.

In a skillet, heat oil over medium-high heat. Add meatloaves and sear for 1 minute on each side. Place on prepared baking sheet. Bake in preheated oven for 40 minutes or until meat is cooked and no longer pink.

Meanwhile, in a small bowl, combine ingredients for yogurt sauce and refrigerate until ready to serve.

Serve one loaf per adult and half or a third per child.

Serve with yogurt sauce, rice and a green vegetable.

• • • • • • • • • • • • • •

VARIATION

You can shape this into meatballs. This requires a bit more manipulation and time than mini loaves, but they are quicker to cook in the oven: about 25 minutes (check that the meat is fully cooked).

BLACK BEAN
Quesadillas

4 servings • **PREPARATION:** 10 minutes • **COOKING TIME:** 20 minutes

INGREDIENTS

1 tbsp + 3 tsp canola oil, divided

1 tbsp ground cumin

1 clove garlic, crushed

1 can (19 oz/540 ml) black beans, drained and rinsed

2 tbsp water

6 whole wheat tortillas, about 6 inches (15 cm)

1½ cups (375 ml) grated old Cheddar cheese

METHOD

In a skillet, heat 1 tbsp of the oil over medium heat. Add cumin and fry for a few seconds. Add garlic and black beans. Stir. Add water, stir and place in a deep dish. (Wash skillet before next step.) Use a fork to coarsely mash beans into a thick purée. Add a bit of water as needed to obtain desired consistency.

On work surface, spread bean mixture over half of each tortilla. Top with grated cheese. Fold tortillas in half.

In clean skillet, heat 1 tsp of oil over medium heat and cook two tortillas for 3 minutes or until bottom is golden. Turn and continue cooking for 3 minutes or until other side is golden. Set aside. Repeat with other tortillas using remaining oil.

On work surface, using a chef's knife or pizza cutter, cut each tortilla into three slices.

Serve with salsa and plain yogurt or sour cream. Accompany tortillas with diced tomatoes and sliced avocado.

4 servings • PREPARATION: 20 minutes • COOKING TIME: 15 minutes

INGREDIENTS

3 tbsp olive oil, divided

½ tsp curry powder

½ tsp grated ginger

½ cup (125 ml) quinoa, rinsed and drained

¾ cup (180 ml) water

1 orange

1 can (19 oz/540 ml) chickpeas, drained and rinsed

½ bulb fennel, finely diced

1 red pepper, finely diced

Pepper

METHOD

In a saucepan, heat 1 tbsp of the oil over medium-high heat. Add curry and ginger and heat for 1 minute. Add quinoa and stir for 1 minute. Add water. Cover and simmer over medium-low heat for 15 minutes or until quinoa is cooked.

Meanwhile, zest the orange, then peel and remove white membrane using a knife. Dice orange, keeping any juice that runs off.

In a large bowl, combine chickpeas, fennel, pepper, orange zest, orange and its juice.

Add quinoa and remaining 2 tbsp of oil. Season with pepper and stir gently.

BABY INFO

Quinoa is one of the best sources of iron among grains.

NORDIC SHRIMP
Risotto

4 servings • PREPARATION: 20 minutes • COOKING TIME: 20 minutes

INGREDIENTS

2 tbsp butter

1 onion, finely chopped

1½ cups (375 ml) Arborio rice

4 cups (1 liter) homemade or
low-sodium chicken broth, hot

¼ cup (60 ml) 15% M.F. cream

1 cup (250 ml) grated Parmesan

1 cup (250 ml) peas, cooked

1½ cups (375 ml) Nordic shrimp, fresh
or defrosted, cooked

Pepper

METHOD

In a saucepan over medium heat, melt butter. Add onion and soften for 3 minutes. Add rice, stirring to coat, and cook for 1 minute.

Add 1 cup (250 ml) of the broth and reduce, stirring constantly, until completely absorbed. Repeat, using 1 cup (250 ml) of broth at a time, until all rice is cooked. (You may need a bit more or a bit less broth.)

Remove from heat to add cream and Parmesan. Add peas and shrimp, stirring gently, and reheat for 5 minutes. Season with pepper.

BABY INFO

Shrimp is high in omega-3 fat, which contributes to the development of the brain, nervous system and eyes. Nordic shrimp are sustainably fished, another good reason to choose them.

CHEESE SANDWICHES
on French Toast

4 servings • PREPARATION: 20 minutes • COOKING TIME: 20 minutes

METHOD

In a bowl with a wide bottom, beat together eggs and milk. Set aside.

In a large nonstick skillet over medium heat, melt 2 tsp butter.

Dip 4 slices of bread in egg mixture. Fry in skillet for about 4 minutes on each side. Transfer to a plate. Repeat with remaining bread and butter.

On a work surface, spread cheese and apples on 4 slices of bread. Cover each slice of bread with another to make sandwiches.

In a skillet, heat sandwiches over medium-high heat for 2 minutes on each side, until cheese has melted. Press down lightly with a spatula. (They can be reheated in a panini press.)

INGREDIENTS

| 3 eggs |
| ½ cup (125 ml) milk |
| 4 tsp butter, divided |
| 8 slices whole wheat bread |
| 1½ cups (375 ml) grated firm cheese (e.g. Cheddar, Swiss cheese) |
| 2 apples, peeled and thinly sliced |

VARIATIONS

- Use raisin bread or Belgian bread instead of whole wheat bread.
- You can use pears instead of apples.
- Use any local cheese. Sandwiches for babies should be made with pasteurized cheese.

FOR ADULTS

Make your sandwiches with nut bread. For variation and a heartier sandwich, you can add ham.

SPAGHETTI WITH TOMATO
and Red Bean Sauce

STARTING AT 9 MONTHS

6 servings • PREPARATION: 15 minutes • COOKING TIME: 20 minutes

INGREDIENTS

1 tbsp olive oil

1 shallot, chopped

2 garlic cloves, crushed

1 can (28 oz/796 ml) crushed tomatoes

1 can (28 oz/796 ml) diced tomatoes with no added salt

½ cup (125 ml) dried tomatoes in oil, not drained, chopped

1 can (19 oz/540 ml) red beans, drained and rinsed, coarsely crushed with a pestle

1 tbsp dried basil

2 tsp dried oregano

Pepper

12 oz (340 g) spaghetti or other long pasta

METHOD

In a saucepan, heat oil over medium-high heat. Add shallot and brown for 2 minutes. Add garlic and continue cooking for 1 minute.

Add crushed tomatoes, diced tomatoes, dried tomatoes and red beans. Bring to a boil, stirring.

Add basil, oregano and pepper. Cover and simmer over low heat for 20 minutes. Add a bit of water as needed.

Meanwhile, in a saucepan over high heat, bring water to a boil. Add pasta and stir to prevent it sticking to the bottom. Cook according to package directions

Serve with vegetables.

. . . .

VARIATION

Use long or short pasta, or even replace wheat pasta with gluten-free, quinoa, rice or corn pasta or bean noodles.

TOFU
with Peanut Sauce

4 servings • PREPARATION: 20 minutes • COOKING TIME: 15 minutes

INGREDIENTS

1 package (15 oz/454 g) firm tofu, cubed

1 tbsp peanut or canola oil

2 carrots, peeled and sliced in thin rounds

2 cups (500 ml) broccoli florets

3 tbsp water

For the sauce

1 cup (250 ml) low-sodium chicken broth

⅓ cup (80 ml) natural creamy peanut butter

1 tbsp lime juice

1 tbsp maple syrup

1 tsp low-sodium soy sauce

1 tsp hoisin sauce

¼ tsp chili paste

Pepper

METHOD

In a saucepan, prepare sauce by combining broth, peanut butter, lime juice, maple syrup, soy sauce, hoisin sauce and chili paste. Heat over medium-high heat, stirring frequently, for 5 minutes or until sauce is blended. Season with pepper. Set aside.

Meanwhile, in a large skillet or wok over high heat, brown tofu cubes in oil for 10 minutes or until crispy and golden on several sides. Set aside.

In same skillet over medium heat, sauté carrots and broccoli for 2 minutes. Add water, cover and cook for 5 minutes or until vegetables are tender.

Return tofu to skillet with vegetables. Add peanut sauce and stir to coat. Adjust seasoning as needed.

Serve with rice or rice vermicelli.

• • • • • • • • • • • • • • •

VARIATION

This peanut sauce can also accompany chicken or spring rolls.

ABOUT
the Author

Stéphanie Côté is a registered dietitian at Extenso, the nutrition research center at Université de Montréal, and for the website Naître et grandir. Eleven years ago, when she was pregnant with her first child, she started specializing in nutrition for children. Since then, her roles as a mother and nutritionist have been mutually feeding each other.

Stéphanie is both a nutritionist and a communicator, basically because she has never been able to choose between the two. In 2000, she was awarded the Fernand-Seguin Fellowship, which recognizes emerging talents in scientific reporting. Since then she has appeared on television, radio, in print and on the web. Stéphanie has had the privilege of learning from the greats, both in journalism and in cooking, in particular Ricardo Larrivée. She owes them a debt of gratitude for a great part of this book.

One of Stéphanie's wishes, or perhaps even missions, is to share the pleasure of eating well with young and old. It seems to be working, because according to her children Laura and Benjamin, **"It's fun having a mother who is a nutritionist, because we like what we eat."**

Stéphanie is a keen athlete, which is why she has developed expertise in the area. She and Philippe Grand co-wrote, *Sports Nutrition*, part of the Know What to Eat collection. Besides, there is a connection between sports and children, because being a mother keeps you running! We wouldn't have it any other way.

stephaniecote.ca

naitreetgrandir.com

nospetitsmangeurs.org

ACKNOWLEDGMENTS

Two for two! In two books, I have been lucky enough to write about my favorite topics in nutrition. The manuscript for *Sports Nutrition* was barely handed in before Groupe Modus asked me to write this book. Thank you, Marc G. Alain and Isabelle Jodoin for your continued trust in me.

A big thanks to Nolwenn Gouezel for her professionalism and perfectionism in copyediting.

Thank you to food stylist Gabrielle Dalessandro and especially photographer André Noël. Beautiful pictures are so important in cookbooks.

Having a nice author's photo is important too, and feeling beautiful in front of the camera helps. Thank you to David Moore for my picture.

Special thanks to my colleagues and friends Philippe Grand and Laurence Chapdelaine who read and commented on the manuscript for the bargain price of a beer.

RESOURCES
for Parents

Health Canada
www.hc-sc.gc.ca/fn-an/nutrition/infant-nourisson/recom/index-eng

Dietitians of Canada
www.dietitians.ca/Dietitians-Views/Prenatal-and-Infant/Infant-Feeding

La Leche League Canada
www.lllc.ca

Centers for Disease Control and Prevention
www.cdc.gov/breastfeeding

Breastfeeding USA
www.breastfeedingusa.org

Naître et Grandir
Authoritative website and magazine for child development
www.naitreetgrandir.com

Nos Petits Mangeurs
Reference center for early childhood nutrition
www.nospetitsmangeurs.org

Maman pour la Vie
www.mamanpourlavie.com

Institut National de Santé Publique du Québec
From Tiny Tot to Toddler: A pratically quide for parents from pregnancy
to age two
www.inspq.qc.ca

Academy of Nutrition and Dietetics
www.eatrigh.org

RECIPE index

KNOW WHAT TO EAT

A diet suited to your needs based on advice from expert dietitians

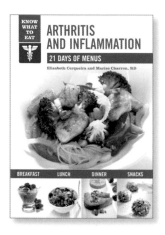

ARTHRITIS AND INFLAMMATION
21 DAYS OF MENUS
Elisabeth Cerqueira and Marise Charron, RD
BREAKFAST · LUNCH · DINNER · SNACKS

BABIES
21 DAYS OF MENUS
Stéphanie Côté, MSc, RD
BREAKFAST · LUNCH · DINNER · SNACKS

DIABETES
21 DAYS OF MENUS
Alexandra Leduc, RD
BREAKFAST · LUNCH · DINNER · SNACKS

IRRITABLE BOWEL SYNDROME
21 DAYS OF MENUS
Alexandra Leduc, RD
BREAKFAST · LUNCH · DINNER · SNACKS

SPORTS NUTRITION
21 DAYS OF MENUS
Stéphanie Côté and Philippe Grand, RD
BREAKFAST · LUNCH · DINNER · SNACKS

WEIGHT LOSS
21 DAYS OF MENUS
Elisabeth Cerqueira and Marise Charron, RD
BREAKFAST · LUNCH · DINNER · SNACKS

MODUSVIVENDIPUBLISHING.COM